GOD,

SEX

&

YOUTH

Books by WILLIAM E. HULME

Face Your Life With Confidence

How to Start Counseling

Counseling and Theology

God, Sex and Youth

GOD, SEX & YOUTH

William E. Hulme

CONCORDIA PUBLISHING HOUSE
SAINT LOUIS   LONDON

The case histories presented in this book are based on actual instances, but any similarity in the names employed in this book to those of persons living or dead is purely coincidental.

First CONCORDIA Paperback edition 1968
Concordia Publishing House, St. Louis, Missouri
Concordia Publishing House Ltd., London, E. C. 1

MANUFACTURED IN THE UNITED STATES OF AMERICA

TO

MY WIFE,

LUCY

whose help in preparing this
book has been indispensable

PREFACE TO PAPERBACK EDITION

There is much talk today about a sexual revolution. We have undergone a liberalization that has emancipated us from old tyrannies that inhibited our freedom to inquire and to question. The trend has also had its distorting effects. Like the swing of a pendulum, emancipation movements tend to react against curtailment by going to the opposite extreme. When this happens, new freedoms are easily abused, and the abuse of freedom creates new bondages.

The changes that are taking place provide the opportunity for teamwork between church, school, home, and youth to discuss the new morality and to avoid the distortions.

As sex education increases in our schools, providing information and understanding on the level of the biological and social sciences, forums for teenagers and their parents are conducted by an increasing number of churches. Here sex can be discussed from the vantage point of God's creative design and values. My hope is that this book and the guide provided in the appendix will be useful for such forums.

We are challenged in our day to provide new ways of approaching an old subject. In speaking of sex with reference to God we are not referring to a code that may become dated from one societal change to another but to a picture of life, a design for relationships, a point of view that transcends societal changes. Youth often believe they know the church's position on these matters, but they do not understand why. Yet when asked to state the church's position they usually refer to prohibitions. This association of religion with the negative and its position on sex with restraint is unfortunate. The implication is that since sex is a pleasure, it is under a cloud of suspicion. This attitude makes the church seem like a parent clamping controls on normal adolescent explorations.

It is good that the church is now taking the initiative to change all this. The Gospel of Christ is good news also in matters of sex. What God has to say about sex is not something to defend but something to proclaim. It is my experience that youth are eager to see this positive picture. The case history style in this book may help the reader to become involved so that he understands the good news for himself. If youth understand the structure, they can apply its principles to their personal situation.

You may wish that I had spelled out more in detail how the principles apply to each personal situation. If I had done so, I would have simply offered a new set of rules and with it, the age-old challenge to find a loophole. We would be back to playing the game, "outwitting the parent." The opportunity provided by the changes in our society would be lost.

I am determined not to let this happen. I want to talk to you as one growing into adulthood, as one who needs to affirm oneself in responsibility and maturity. If you desire further details, go to a pastoral counselor. This book, though presented in dialogue form, is not meant to be a substitute for an actual relationship. In a counseling relationship you can discuss your needs in an atmosphere that encourages responsibility rather than resistance.

WILLIAM E. HULME
April 2, 1968

Contents

1

Let's Be Frank

A Story from Life

Cheryl Sanders was a sensitive girl. You didn't have
to look twice to know that something was bothering her.

"It's about Jack and me," she said. "I just don't know
what to do."

"Suppose you tell me about it," I said.

"Well—you know a lot of it," she said. "But I'll begin at
the beginning anyhow. Jack—as you know—had very
little interest in religion before I started to go with him."
Cheryl paused as though questioning how to go further.

"Yes, I remember," I said.

"I wanted to help him," she said. "He was so mixed up.
His folks aren't good to him the way mine are to me. I
felt that God had laid his soul on my heart—that I was
supposed to help him."

Again she paused. This time I remained silent.

Finally she spoke. "And I think I have. But—now I am
failing." Cheryl's eyes began to get watery. "Jack and I
have gone with each other for almost three years. Jack

says he loves me very much—that he will never love anyone else."

"And you?"

"My love for him is growing. But I feel we are both
too young to know whether or not we are in love."

What may begin as a simple boy-girl friendship often
ends up in something more, at least for one of the parties.
Cheryl's strong desire to help Jack spiritually—as fine as
it was—opened the door for a natural romantic involvement.

"How old are you now, Cheryl?" I asked.

"We have both just turned eighteen."

"Then you began to go steady at fifteen," I said.

"We know now it was too young," she said. "But that's
over and gone. What are we going to do now?"

"How do you mean?" I asked.

"Well—I'll get down to the problem. Lately—for about
five or six months we have gotten too—too physically
intimate."

"I see."

"I have a lot of will power but not quite enough," she
said.

"And Jack?"

"He knows that being so emotional is wrong, but he says
he just can't help it. We have gotten so that we do quite
a bit of petting. We both feel terrible afterwards."

"Your conscience bothers you?"

"We talk it over and try to reason everything out," she
said, "but we are just so mixed up we don't know what to
do."

"You feel like you are up against a stone wall."

"Yes," she said. "We have read the Bible together and

prayed, trying to get help, but it's so hard." She fought to keep back the tears. "I pray to God asking for forgiveness, but then we let ourselves go again. Can God forgive us when we do things like this?"

"You mean, when you ask for forgiveness and then do the same things over again?"

"Yes," she said. "I get so that I cry a lot because I feel so bad. I don't know how I could have gotten into such a hopeless state."

"You don't see any way out?"

"We could get married, I suppose," she said. "I'm just not sure about myself—how I feel about Jack. He insists that he will always love me. But how do you know when you haven't really gone with anybody else? I feel we are both too young to know."

"You don't feel you are old enough to make such a long-lasting decision," I said.

Cheryl looked even glummer than before. "What can we do about these emotions of ours?" she said, without taking her eyes off the floor. "I get so confused."

Cheryl is confused for a good reason. She feels that both she and Jack are too young to know whether they are in love. At the same time they have allowed their affection for each other to push them into a situation which is becoming harder and harder to live with.

A Problem in Sex?

We could call this a problem in sex. We could also call it a problem of courtship—of going steady—or even of religion. How could you suggest that we help Cheryl and Jack? Suppose Cheryl had come to you. Or even suppose you *are* Cheryl—or Jack. What would you suggest as a wise course of action? Would you suggest that they break up? Do you think they have the will power to carry out such a decision? Suppose they are meant for each other. Perhaps you would suggest that they marry. What about their youth and seeming immaturity? And then there is Cheryl's own hesitancy as to whether she is sure about her feelings for Jack.

Maybe you believe they could discipline themselves more. They say they have tried. What practical suggestions could you give them to carry out this discipline? Would double-dating help? What if the other couple has the same problem? How about not seeing each other so often? Then they may only think about each other all the more.

Do you think they should date other persons too? The trouble is that all their friends believe they are going steady, and the other boys won't date Cheryl for this reason. And Jack says he is so much in love that he could not think of asking anyone else for a date. Even if they date other persons, could the same problem occur all over again with somebody else?

Could they continue as they are? What about their conscience? Is it wrong? What is the will of God on such things as heavy petting? Is there any harm in becoming so physically intimate in dating?

Perhaps you think that all I have done is confuse you. If so, I assure you that this is not my only purpose. It is questions such as these that we have raised about Cheryl and Jack which we are going to discuss in this book. We are going to try to find some answers, too. Together we are going to look into the Christian view of sex and see how it relates to our life with others, and with ourselves, and to our future.

Frankness, Reverence, Maturity

There are three adjectives that I would like to use as guides to our discussion.

The first of these is *frankness*. There is little use in talking about this subject if we are going to cloak our thoughts in words that are vague and confusing. For the sake of clarity it is necessary to speak frankly, even about intimate things. I am sure you want it this way, for otherwise we would only be wasting our time.

The second adjective is *reverence*. We are going to approach the subject of sex as a creation of God. Therefore in all that we investigate we are beholding His handiwork. We are searching for His purposes in His creation. Whether we refer to the body, the mind or the soul, we shall do so in the spirit of reverence for life as God has created it.

The third adjective is *maturity*. I am going to take for granted that you are grown up enough to deal with this subject frankly and reverently. And you *will* be as long as you remember that there is nothing in God's creation that need embarrass you if you approach it with reverence. Perhaps you have heard the subject of sex discussed before in ways that made you uncomfortable. This was due to the *manner* in which it was talked about rather than the subject itself.

Let us begin our search by looking into the way that God has created us. If God is good, then the way He made us is good also. With this in mind let us turn to the next chapter.

2

How It All Started

Without being clairvoyant I know that I have two kinds of readers. And I know that *you* belong to one of these kinds. You are either male or female.

This division in the human family goes back to our creation. In the Bible story of this creation the man was created first, and by himself he was lonely. Although he could give names to the other forms of creation—the birds of the air and the beasts of the field—he could find in none of them the companionship that he craved. Alone, he was not complete. In a sense his longing for companionship was a prayer to the Creator. And God who "is able to do far more abundantly than all that we ask or think," [1] did not answer Adam's need as Adam may have thought; that is, by giving him another person like himself. Rather He gave him one who could meet his need for companionship far more deeply than another man. He gave him woman.

[1] Ephesians 3:20

Adam Was Lonely

When Adam saw the woman he said, "This at last is bone of my bones and flesh of my flesh." [2] Here was one who was like him, and yet in a wonderful way was still different. Woman in her difference completes man, and man completes woman. When we think of man we think of those qualities that go with masculinity—physical strength, aggressive spirit, protection of the home. When we think of woman we think of the feminine—strength in the form of tenderness, warmth in her bearing—the one who gives the "feeling tone" to the home.

Actually every man has some qualities of femininity within him, but in a lesser way; that is, he is a man. So also every woman has qualities of masculinity to a degree, but she abounds in femininity, for she is a woman. When they come together in the union of marriage, they more or less complete each other and form a unit. It is something like two halves coming together to make a whole. Each is the complement of the other. And so God has made possible this deepest companionship on earth, as the two become one—one flesh, one mind, one spirit. It is expressed in a humorous and yet touching way in this poem:

> Come back Eva, I've relented,
> All I said was just invented
>   By demented
>   Jealousy,
> Love gone crazy. Here's a handsome
> Frank confession; for my ransom
>   Come and plant some
>   Sense in me.

2 Genesis 2:23

Day by day I've no one sharing
Home and garden, no one caring
    What I'm wearing.
        Life began
Not with Adam; when the new man
Lived alone, he wasn't human:
    Adam's woman
        Made him man.[3]

This is the Christian definition of sex: that God created
people as men and women for the purpose of the marriage
companionship and the creation and development of new
life. "For this cause a man shall leave his father and
mother and be joined to his wife, and the two shall become one. So they are no longer two but one."[4]

Sex is a good word. Nevertheless it has degenerated so
far from its Christian context that it is often embarrassing
for some persons even to use the word in "polite" society.
Yet we all know that it is frequently used without embarrassment in "other than polite" societies. The reason
for this is that there are other definitions of sex than the
Christian one.

Differing Ideas About Sex

The idea rather common in these "other than polite"
societies is that sex is a means for having some fun. But
fun is taken here in its most selfish meaning. People who
use sex for self-centered pleasure, *use* others rather than
respect them. They think of people as bodies rather than
as persons. Naturally this animal-like view of sex is offensive to many. The result is a reaction in the opposite direction. Unfortunately these reactions, though motivated by

[3] By William Force Stead. Printed originally in *Harper's Magazine*.
[4] Genesis 2:24

religious ideals, can be as unchristian as the abuses they are attempting to remedy.

Correcting abuses can be compared to the movement of a pendulum. When the pendulum swings to the left, and then starts to return to the right, it does not stop at the middle of its course, but is carried by its momentum an equal distance in the opposite direction. So it often happens that well-meaning people go to the opposite extreme when they fight abuses. Sometimes it is people who have had sordid experiences with sex in the past who tend to go beyond the middle in their reforms. In the history of the Church St. Augustine is an example of this tendency. When our experience with sex has been degrading, it is difficult for us (emotionally, at least) to accept sex as something that can also be pure. Yet the Bible is very clear at this point. "Everything created by God is good, and nothing is to be rejected if it is received with thanksgiving, for then it is consecrated by the Word of God and by prayer." [5]

When people go to the opposite extreme, they may feel that sex is at best a necessary evil. Naturally we have to reproduce the race, and therefore people must marry. But for those who want to live the highest kind of God-pleasing life, even marriage is out.

Others may feel that sex is a biological necessity for the reproduction of the race, and therefore marriage and a God-pleasing life even in its highest sense go together. Yet any purpose for sex beyond reproductive purposes is only tolerated by the Creator, and is best kept to a minimum. These people would be ashamed to acknowledge that they receive any pleasure from sexual experience in marriage. Creation itself has become suspect. The prin-

[5] I Timothy 4:3

ciple seems to be that it is wrong to enjoy what some people abuse.

Redeeming the Word Sex

In such religious views as these, sex is obviously never fully accepted into a spiritual view of life. It is on the outside of the "sacred," a telltale reminder that so far as our physical passions are concerned, we are still very much related to the lower animals.

Here, it seems to me, is one of the biggest victories the Devil has accomplished. God created sex in man as something distinctly human and something good. While it is physical, it is also spiritual. But people have always had a hard time accepting the Creator's wisdom. Either they accept sex as purely biological and glory in it, or they accept it purely as physical and apologize for it. As a result the notions of sex we hear in daily conversation usually come from people with a very low appreciation of the spiritual side of sex. These are our "sex educators." People who should be talking about sex in its Christian meaning have treated it as a subject of taboo—an unmentionable. And so the Devil has a field day.

Let us redeem the word "sex" by using it rightly. The best way to defeat the negative is to crowd it out with the positive.

On the lawn of the school where I teach we have beautiful grass. I had often marveled at it and one day I asked the custodian how he accomplished it. "I suppose that you use a lot of spray to kill the weeds."

"No," he said, "I don't. I just keep sowing more grass seed until finally the weeds are all crowded out." This is the way to "overcome evil with good."

Growing into Differences

You are growing into the differences that characterize manhood and womanhood. Some of you have already arrived, some may be just beginning, and some may be in the midst of it. If girls could watch some of their boy friends study their own faces in their mirrors, they would be highly amused. For the boys are searching for some evidence on their faces of the beginning of a whisker. And when they find it—and it may only be "peach fuzz" —it makes them happy. Why shouldn't it? They are growing into manhood, and this is good and wholesome.

A boy's voice may be still high like a girl's. On the other hand it may have already changed into its distinctly masculine tenor, or baritone or bass. But worst of all, it may be in that in-between stage where it shoots off in all directions. The boy never knows when he starts out on one pitch where he will end up. And this is embarrassing to him. His unmanageable voice is symbolic of the whole process of awkwardness that often accompanies these changing functions in adolescence.

Girls are also noticing changes in themselves. They are going from girlhood into womanhood. The shape of their bodies is developing into the contour of their mothers' bodies. Inside their bodies the process that is associated with the woman's ability to bear children has begun. This is the menstrual cycle, which causes girls to have a "period" about once a month. And all of this is God-designed—wholesome and good.

Not all young people develop at the same rate. Perhaps you have felt that others in your grade at school are more advanced than you are in these changes that I have mentioned. This is entirely possible. Not everyone at age fifteen is in the same stage of development from boyhood into manhood or from girlhood into womanhood. The time at which these changes begin to occur, and the rate at which they develop, is largely determined by your heredity. Some people's heredity predestines them to an early physical maturation and others to a slower one. If you are somewhat irritated at being behind the others, the main thing for you to remember is that you will arrive. You need not be anxious. God is at work.

In this change from boyhood into manhood and girlhood into womanhood there are developing those organs designed for marriage—the sex organs. Through these the union of husband and wife is experienced physically in marriage. This physical union has several names: the marital or sex relationship, sexual intercourse, or coitus. It is symbolic of the total union of marriage—the union of body, soul, and mind of two people who love each other and have become partners in the creation of a home.

The Marvel of God's Love

Here now we see the marvel of God's love. This union which God has designed—through which husband and wife express their love to each other in a uniquely intimate manner—He has also chosen as the means for the creation of new life. And He has chosen this union of marriage, with its atmosphere of love, to create a home in which the new child can be raised to maturity.

In God's planning, children are conceived and nurtured in love. It is in the security of this atmosphere of loving relationships that the child experiences the love of God. We know from our study of the sciences of humanity that it is through loving relationships within the home that a child develops into a healthy and wholesome personality. How can we help being overcome by a sense of reverence for life and for God when we contemplate the wisdom in the divine design of sex and marriage and family!

3

The Desire to Date

The Change in Attractions

If you are a boy, I am sure you feel entirely different about girls from the way you felt when you were in the second or third grade. My own little boy, who is eight years old, is very conscious of the fact that he is a boy and wants nothing to do with girls. Recently he paid his mother the highest compliment she probably will ever receive. He snuggled up to her and said, "Mom, you're not like a girl to me, you're like a boy."

But I'm pretty sure he isn't going to stay this way. Some day—and the time seems to be coming earlier and earlier —he is going to look at girls quite differently. In a similar way my nine-year-old girl will look in a different way at boys when she becomes a teenager than she does now.

What causes this difference? The same thing that is taking place in your bodies is taking place also in your minds. You are changing from boyhood into manhood and from girlhood into womanhood, not only physically but in your whole person.

These feelings of attraction that you have toward members of the opposite sex are natural and good. A loving and wise God would not cause one part of you to grow to maturity and leave another part way behind. Our body, mind, and spirit function as a unit. When you are drawn toward members of the opposite sex and want to be with them, the divine design is working itself out in your life.

The Selective Process

Out of this attraction comes the desire to date. Certain members of the opposite sex become more attractive to you than others. You want to spend time with them—to do things together. This is the selective process at work in its earliest beginnings. As time goes on, your choice may narrow even more until you find yourself in a "steady" relationship with one person. And then there is engagement and finally marriage.

In between the desire to date and a steady courtship with one person there is a period known as social dating. In this period of our development we form fellowships and date with a variety of young people of the opposite sex. This is a good experience for our development. Dating with different people is a broadening experience socially. Through it we learn to relate to people as men and women and in so doing learn to relate to ourselves. In this sense it is good preparation for the later experience of marriage.

But it is precisely here that we face a problem. This period of social dating is threatened by our current practice of "going steady" at a very early age. Not only are we going steady earlier than the previous generation, but we are dating earlier, and as a result, marrying earlier.

Pressures to Go Steady

As you know only too well, there are a lot of pressures on young people to go steady at an early age. First there are the external pressures. These come primarily from the school setting. In some of our high schools the practice of going steady is so common that you practically lose your social standing if you are not "pinned." In some areas this tendency extends even into the Junior High schools. Those who want to date different people in this setting find the going rather rough. As one girl said, "If you're seen with a boy a couple of times, everybody thinks you're going steady. And you might as well because it's hard to get any dates once it gets around that you're going steady."

Then there are internal pressures. Going steady gives us a kind of security. For one thing when we have a steady boy friend or girl friend we are not so anxious about whom we are going with to the next school function or whether we are going to have a date at all. There is also within some of us a great need for affection and an equally great fear of not getting it—of being alone. Going steady is one way of satisfying this need and of quieting this fear. Perhaps you know the young person who goes from one steady relationship to another, seemingly unable to enter the social arena without this support.

Getting Ahead of Schedule

If we are going to restore social dating to its rightful place in our development, it is obvious we have a pretty big trend to counter. First let us look at some of the problems involved in going steady so early.

It is no coincidence that along with our trend toward early steady relationships we also have a trend toward early marriage. Going steady so young causes the whole process toward the marital goal to get ahead of schedule. After a couple has gone steady for a few years, they become physiologically and psychologically ready for marriage. There would be nothing wrong with this procedure if all of our other faculties matured at the same rate. But normally they do not. And so a couple may find themselves quite settled on marriage before their natural processes of evaluation have reached their adult fulfillment. They are sincere when they say they love each other and know they will never change. The only trouble is they do not know what the next few years are going to do to them.

Once when I mentioned this factor to a group of young people to whom I was speaking, a young couple came up to me at the close of the program. They looked quite crestfallen as they held hands supportingly.

"What you said has us worried," the girl said. "We love each other very much and plan to marry some day. When I finish high school I plan to go to college. Bob is going to farm. Do you think that—that there is a danger that we may never get married?"

"If you plan to go to college," I answered, "you will naturally begin to think in terms of this new experience. If Bob devotes himself to farming, he will not be able to share your experience, nor you his. Nobody can say for sure that you will not marry some day, but your courtship is probably in for some rough going."

"Not us," she said, determinedly—"It won't happen to us."

Several years later I happened to visit with the young

couple's minister. "Tell me," I said, "are Nancy and Bob still going with each other?"

"It's just about over," he said. "Nancy is in her last year of college. She is trying to break it off without hurting Bob too much. But he's taking it awfully hard."

Now let us take a look at it from the other end. I was counseling with a man who had been married twenty years. He wanted to divorce his wife. Things had not worked out as he had planned and hoped they would, and he felt that he did not love her any more. As understandingly as I could, I brought out the fact that in the marriage vow he had taken, he promised "for better or for worse," and that this was probably the "worse."

"I was only eighteen when I was married," he said. "I was really too young to know. Should I be held for the rest of my life to a mistake that I made when I was just a kid?"

Now, of course, this same thing could happen to people who had married later, or it could have been a happy marriage even though they had married very young. The point is that the teen years are developing years and decisions made then about lifelong situations are subject to change as individuals mature. This needs to be said in spite of the fact that people differ to some extent in their rate of development and that girls mature a little sooner than do boys.

Having Your Fun

When young people go from the desire for dating too quickly into a steady relationship which eventually ends in marriage, there is the danger that as the years go by and the responsibilities and burdens of family life begin to weigh heavily, one or both of them may begin to long for the "carefree" days of youth. They may come to regret the fact that they married before they "had their fun." "How did I know if I really loved him?" the woman may ask herself. "I never really went with anybody else!"

These times of being overcome by the "weariness of it all" do not happen only to couples who marry early. Yet when they do occur in such marriages there is the possibility that secret regrets over having been tied down so early may aggravate the revolt. Such people may feel that they have missed something in their life. They want to go back and live out the carefree experience of social dating which they missed. Nature has a way of protesting sooner or later when significant areas in our development are by-passed. Then we seem to need to return and capture the missing experience.

Fear of Spinsterhood

Of course there are complications in the other direction also. In the life of many girls there is a real fear of spinsterhood. Unfortunately our society has placed a stigma on what it calls "being an old maid." To avoid this fate, girls may hesitate to break up their steady relationships, even though otherwise they may believe it is the wise thing to do.

An attractive high school senior counseled with me about whether or not she should discontinue going steady with her boy friend. She was planning to go away to college in the fall, and felt it would be unwise to tie herself down to a boy friend back home. She was not really ready to think about marriage and wanted to make the most out of her college experience socially as well as academically.

Having been associated with a college campus, I could

see the wisdom in her thinking. Yet something was still bothering her. When it finally came out, I was amazed to hear this attractive girl say, "It's just that—well—I guess every girl feels this way—but nobody wants to end up an old maid. Silly isn't it—but you can't know for sure whether you'll ever get another chance."

Naturally she has a point. No one can know for sure when a relationship is broken up, whether another will ever take its place. All we can say is that normally it does. And there may be some who feel that she should remain tied down during her college years in order to be sure. Yet I believe this fear of spinsterhood is as much a hindrance to our becoming married as it is to our maturity.

The more anxious we are to get married, the less attractive we become to the opposite sex. Also this anxiety may lead us into premature steady relationships, engagement and even marriage before we are emotionally mature enough to handle them.

Not Just Marriage but Good *Marriage*

Yet in breaking up a steady relationship, may we not be breaking up a good thing? Although a young couple may be by their own admission too young for marriage, perhaps they can work it out successfully. Yet our experience with life seems to weigh more heavily on the other side.

The mere fact that a couple ceases to go steady is not proof that their relationship is forever severed. In fact, the opposite has frequently happened. These same people who break up because of their youth may later resume their relationship when they can carry it to its natural fulfillment. If our love is as unchangeable as we like to think it is, then this would be the most likely thing to happen.

Even in our early dating the long range goal should be in our thinking. The big issue is not simply marriage, but a *good* marriage. And to this end our wise planning is in terms of our wholesome development as mature men and women.

4

The Marks of Affection

When should a boy and girl kiss?

Is petting wrong?

These are the questions that come up whenever the subject of boy and girl relationships is discussed. They show that when members of the opposite sex have an attraction for each other, there is a desire for a physical expression of this attraction. The same situation is also true in reverse. If a person is repulsive to us, we are loath to touch him.

Desire for Physical Contact

Affection and tenderness are characteristics of the spirit. Yet they are incompletely communicated without the bodily touch. Sex has its deeply spiritual significance, but it is inseparably associated with the functions of the physical. When a boy and a girl are strongly attracted to each other, they want to experience a deeper involvement with each other and they are likely to express this desire in physical ways.

Not all cultures go about their love-making in the same

way. If we were Eskimos we would rub noses with our boy friend or girl friend. If we were natives of India we would not have to worry about the problem at all, for our parents would make all the necessary arrangements for our marriage, even to the selection of the mate. In our culture the marks of affection center in the kiss and embrace. The question is when should they be used? On the first date? The second? Or should one wait until the fifth or sixth?

When Should We?

When we ask for the Christian answer to such questions we cannot expect a set of directions as if we were operating a machine. Cut and dried rules for every situation would simplify things, but they would also violate the freedom of personality and the uniqueness of each individual.

The Christian answer takes into consideration both our freedom and our complexity. What we are on the outside cannot be separated from what we are on the inside. In other words, if we want the Christian answer we have to examine and consider our motives.

The kiss and the embrace are signs of endearment. True, they are sometimes used as mere formalities. When you have to kiss your aunt you may feel this is strictly a duty. But when these signs are used between a young man and young woman in a dating relationship, they symbolize the attraction that exists between them. They are marks of affection.

When should we use them in our dating? The answer must come from our inner self. When we use them in line with their meaning—when we are honest in our feelings of affection for the other person—they are good.

Like everything else the kiss and embrace can be abused as well as used. While I was pastoral counselor to college students I was impressed by what I call the "great illusion." Girls would come to me with this complaint: "These boys! Honestly! They expect you to let them kiss you on the first night. And if you don't—then you don't get any more dates!"

When the boys came they had this story: "These girls! Man alive! They expect you to try and kiss them on the first date. And if you don't, they think you're green behind the ears or something. And you don't get any more dates!"

There it is! Each is trying to live up to what he or she thinks the other expects. It is bad enough that each has misinterpreted the expectations of the other. But what is worse is that neither is being himself. Neither is being honest.

Some argue that kissing and embracing in dating are small matters, but we have here an example of how little things are really big things. The alternative to sincerity lies somewhere in the direction of dishonesty—and selfishness. To play fast and loose with the kiss and the embrace in order to live up to expectations, or to build a reputation as a "fast" date, or for the "fun" of a sexual stimulation, is to do harm to ourselves—to say nothing of what we may be doing to the other person. Honesty here contributes positively to our whole personality development. It is a needed exercise in character building at a time when character is being molded.

When Tom came to see me he was not sure about his feelings toward Helen. "I like to date her and all that," he said. "But I don't want her to take me seriously, because I don't know whether I feel about her *that* way or not."

"Well," I said, "it would seem to me that you should be honest with Helen and let her know how you feel."

"Oh, I've done that," he said. "I've told her. But evidently she wants to keep going with me anyhow."

Some months later Helen was in my office. She was very upset. "Tom's quit going with me," she said. "I can't understand it. He seemed so sincere."

"Didn't he tell you how he felt?" I asked.

"Oh, yes," she said, "he told me not to take him seriously —but his actions didn't back up his words."

Tom thought that because he was honest with Helen in what he *said*, he could still have his "fun" in what he *did*. But actions speak louder than words to many people. The problem was that Helen liked Tom, and when she had to choose between what he said and what he did, she chose the latter. The result was a very hurt young lady.

How Much Affection?

The next question is—how much affection? Granted that honesty should guide us in our use of the marks of affection, how involved in them should we become?

This is a good question for the simple reason that one kiss makes us want another, and the kiss itself tends to become more and more intense in its expression of emotion. This intensity we call passion. There is quite a difference between a perfunctory peck on the cheek or even on the lips, and a prolonged and passionate embrace.

To answer the question "how much?," we need to see what happens to us when we increase the tempo and extent of our love making. First of all, pronounced bodily changes take place. The heart beats faster; the blood pressure goes up; more adrenalin goes into the blood stream. Our whole being grows in excitement. We are in a big buildup, obviously headed for a destination. In its final sense this destination is the marital union.

In spite of our convictions that this experience belongs within the marriage relationship, there is the danger that when this buildup reaches a certain momentum, the excitement of our emotions may overwhelm our good sense as well as our powers of discipline. We may experience the marital union outside of the marriage relationship. We would then experience the symbol without the thing it symbolizes. Doing this destroys the divine design of sex. It undermines the harmony and order of social living.

The Sex Union and Marriage

It is evident from the Bible that the sexual union is a serious thing. St. Paul says that he who joins himself even to a prostitute becomes one body with her. It indicates a union of persons that only people who live as married people can realize.

This does not mean that simply by becoming married, people will use the sexual union as God designed it. Not all people who are married outwardly are really married in spirit. But it does mean that only people who live in a married relationship can experience the partnership in living that the sexual union expresses, namely, the utter need of one for the other that "two becoming one" signifies.

The Bible also refers to the sexual act as an act of *knowing* each other. It is difficult to put into words what is meant by *know*. There is a mystery about sex. But in the union that takes place each of the partners is privileged to enter into a very personal and intimate knowledge about the other and about himself. There is a sense of permanence to such a union of "knowing." It can rightly belong only to those who have committed themselves to each other.

If this union occurs before the commitment of marriage, is it the result of love? Some persons think so. "Their love was too strong for them to control," they say. Is this love or a romantic substitute for love? Let us explore into the situation to find out.

There is naturally a big difference between a promiscuous type of relationship where the individuals involved care little for each other as persons, and the experience of the sexual union between sweethearts who love each other. The attitudes are entirely different. Yet even in the case of the latter it is questionable whether love itself would cause them to have sexual relationships. To test this we need to judge the matter not only on the basis of our feelings but also on the basis of our thinking. The question is whether one is seeking the best interests of his or her beloved in encouraging sexual union before marriage? Or is it a matter of trying to justify our immediate desires when our concern about future values is at a low ebb?

If we understand what is involved, I believe we can see that our love for the other person, and even for ourselves, would reserve the marital union for the time of marriage. Is it love to influence our friend to enter into a sacred expression of union when he or she is not able to assume the responsibilities involved in such a union? Would this not be the same as encouraging him to be something less than honest? Or the same as encouraging him to go against the Creator's plan? Particularly when we realize the danger that bad effects rather than good effects may result?

What does one do if he finds himself face to face with temptation? Bob Anderson had such an experience. Perhaps we could profit by letting him tell us about it. We got onto the subject indirectly, for Bob was usually tight-lipped about himself. It was after a young people's gathering at Church where the subject of Christian sexual ethics had been discussed. The two of us happened to be the last ones to leave.

"There was one point I wanted to bring up tonight," he said rather hesitatingly, "but you know how it is—it's hard for me to speak in a group. The point I wanted to make was—it isn't always the fellow that makes the advances."

"No?" I asked. "You mean the girls have to be watched too?"

"That's right," he said. "I—I know."

"Oh?"

"Well—I guess it's on my mind because it just happened a couple of weeks ago. That is—I had an experience along these lines."

"Would you like to tell me about it?"

"Yeah, I kind of would," he said. "It's bothered me some since. I'd been going on and off with this girl. I wouldn't want to mention her name. I kind of liked her. We—ah—smooched some. And then this one night—I guess maybe I was a little too amorous—but I said something like—'I wish we were married.'"

I simply nodded and he went on.

"And she said—'I do too.' And then—like a bolt out of the blue she said—'You don't have to be married to me.' I wasn't sure I heard right, so all I could say was—'What?' Then she said it again—'You don't have to be married to me.' With that she kind of went limp against me. My head started spinning, believe me. Here she was —giving me the green light."

Again I thought it best just to nod.

"Well—I sort of hesitated. I guess she thought I needed a push—for the next thing I heard was, 'Take me, Bob.' I'm telling you, right then and there you've got to face what you really believe!"

"In other words the issue was perfectly clear."

"I'm not saying I didn't have a tussle," he said. "But in a way I'm glad it *was* clear. I think it helped me to know what I should do."

"And what *did* you do, Bob?"

"Well—all kinds of feelings went through me. I think I was even scared for a moment. Then I wanted to push her away. I guess I was kind of disgusted with her. But I think the thing that finally came to me was—how can I do the right thing here and still not humiliate her. It seemed like hours but I imagine it was only a matter of seconds. I said, 'You must think quite a bit of me.' By this time I was ready for anything."

"Did she answer?"

"She kind of purred—I think she said, 'I do.' I told her, 'I think a lot of you too. But I think it will be better for us if we didn't.' "

I waited for him to continue.

"She just stayed quiet. I felt I had to say something more. So I said something like this—'It's just that—well —I believe that God would be much happier with both of us if we controlled ourselves.' "

"What was the outcome?"

"She drew back and acted a little piqued," he said. "I took her home shortly after. She still wasn't saying much. Maybe she was even relieved—I don't know. Anyhow I've seen her since a couple of times. We just act like nothing had happened."

"How do you feel toward her now?" I asked.

"I lost some respect for her, but I try not to show it. I don't want to hurt her. I just hope that—maybe the experience was good for both of us."

When young people who have respect for God and for each other experience the sexual union before marriage, there is at least subconsciously a loss in their sense of honor and of respect for themselves and the other person. Instead of wholesome attitudes and feelings developing around the sex act, there is the likelihood that the destructive emotions of guilt and anxiety and even of resentment will become associated with it. These may carry over into the marriage relationship. It is difficult to incorporate sex into the spiritual life if it is handicapped by these negative impressions. In terms of the best interests of the couple's future, it is not their love, but rather their weakness or their selfishness, that causes them to want sexual union before they are ready for marriage.

Problems in Heavy Indulgence

Not all people are overpowered by the heightened emotions of love making. Some have a greater discipline over themselves than others. Still others may not have so great a need for affection. (As we shall see later these two often go together.)

Some couples may find that they can indulge heavily in the marks of affection without actually entering into the sexual union itself. Yet they experience the same buildup of emotions within themselves. They are preparing for the same climax, and since the climax is not forthcoming, the buildup of excitation is left unsatisfied. This leads to a continual frustration.

Also the energy they generate by the love-making is pent up inside them. It does not evaporate. Since it is not released outwardly it goes to work inwardly. They become jumpy and easily irritated. This leads to quarreling. Small things that normally would cause little concern now become occasions for expressing the negative feelings within them. Each becomes the scapegoat for the other's irritation.

The danger is that these quarrels may become so frequent and intense that they cause the couple to break up. Unfortunately, when this happens they may not realize where the trouble really lies. I have seen several fine romances that might have matured into fine marriages break up in the courtship phase because of petty bickering brought on by an overindulgence in the physical demonstration of affection.

When Edna came to see me she was quite upset about her schoolwork. She could not concentrate and had failed her last three tests. As she talked it became apparent that she had been hurt. I asked her if anything had happened of late that had disturbed her. She did not answer right away, but her look revealed she knew what it was.

"As you might know—it's a guy," she said softly. "We broke up about a month ago. I don't know—I haven't been able to make much sense since. Everything's so mixed up."

"You thought a lot of the fellow," I said.

"I did—I still do. He's going with somebody else now. But I can't seem to forget him. Maybe it's because of the way we broke up. No—it's not just that. The whole thing is a painful memory. I wish—but then it's too late now."

"What do you wish, Edna?"

"Oh—that we would have done things differently. We went at it too hot and heavy. It was real though. We talked of marriage a lot. But all we did was pet."

"You had no other dating activities?"

"Oh, we might go to a show—but even then we—well —you know—were pretty close. But often we didn't even go to a show. To make matters worse we saw each other almost constantly."

"You feel you overdid it."

"I do now," she said. "In a way I guess I did then too— but Danny seemed to like it—and—well, it just seemed that this is what we wanted to do. Then one night—we were on the porch—and my dad came up. He didn't say anything—just cleared his throat. Of course he saw us. But Danny got real embarrassed. It seems that from then on nothing seemed to please him. He'd snap at me for hardly any reason. Naturally I didn't like that. I found myself snapping right back at him. Toward the end, though, I just cried when we quarreled. I knew we were drifting apart but I didn't know what to do about it."

"You believe the change began with that night on the porch."

"No—I really think that's when it came to a head," she said. "I noticed little things before that. A couple of times that week Danny didn't seem his old self when he arrived for our date—almost as if he would just as soon not have come. But we were soon at it—petting, that is—and then he seemed all right again."

"But you are wondering whether he wasn't losing some of his interest even then."

"I know how *I* felt sometimes after he'd gone—sort of ashamed."

"As if you had spoiled a good thing by overdoing it."

"Yes—I can see it so plainly now," she said. "But then it just seemed that everything was going to pieces for no reason. No matter what I would say or do—it would irritate him."

"How did it finally come to an end?" I asked.

"It couldn't have gone on much longer because I was crying most of the time. But the thing that did it was he started going out with another girl. He was open about it, though. He told me that he and she seemed to have more things to talk about than we did."

"I imagine that hurt."

"It did," she said. "But I knew it would be something like that. I'm not a very good conversationalist—don't seem to be able to talk about lots of subjects like some kids."

"You feel inadequate along these lines."

"Yes I do," she said. "I always have. I hadn't thought of this before, but I believe now that's why I was content to pet most of the time. I felt in this way I—that is—that Danny was enjoying my company."

Instead of being an effective compromise between having sex relations and remaining unsatisfied, heavy petting adds fuel to the fire. It is in the very nature of love-making that the further we go in the intensity and intimacy of our expression, the greater is the momentum of our desire for more. This is why young people find it difficult to backtrack in their show of affection once they have become heavy indulgers. The fact is that we can have just as much satisfaction and less frustration in a courtship that is guided by a moderate show of affection than in one that has tried to find something better in heavy indulgence.

There are other complications in a courtship of heavy indulgence. The young lovers are likely to have a sense of guilt about their love-making. The next day when their passion has subsided and their ability to think rationally has returned, they may feel they have been too intimate. Although they have not experienced the actual sexual union, they have been in the area that immediately precedes this union.

It is even possible that the intensity of the love-making may bring on the climax of the union—called orgasm—without any union of organs as such. When we go beyond the moderate kiss and embrace into those areas and intimacies of expression that we call heavy petting, we are in the "lead-up" to the marital union. While technically speaking we are not violating the divine design, we are violating the *spirit* of that design—and we know it. As the immediate buildup for the marital union, this area belongs to the marriage relationship also.

The days of dating are changing days. The boy or girl we are madly in love with during one season we may tire of in the next. If, however, we have allowed ourselves to become too intimate while we were madly in love, we may feel a sense of obligation to the person even when our ardor cools. The more sincere a person is, the more conscientious he is about the feelings of others. So a person may find himself involved in a relationship he would like to terminate, but feels he cannot without being some sort of a "heel." It is not hard to see the unhappy situation this could lead to.

Such an unhappy situation is the theme of William Inge's play, *Come Back, Little Sheba*. It is the story of Doc, a chiropractor in early middle age, and his wife Lola. Doc had a promising future as a young college student studying medicine. Then he met Lola. She was young and pretty, and Doc became infatuated with her. But she was also a very simple girl and no match for Doc's wider interests. Yet the young man's attraction was strong, and with what he later felt was a *too ready* cooperation from Lola, he had gone too far in his love-making. Feeling a sense of obligation to Lola for what had happened, Doc married her.

Their baby died at birth, and Lola could never have any children afterward. Doc changed to chiropractic because under the circumstances he could not complete medical school. Their differences in interests soon became obvious. In his disillusionment with life Doc took to drink. Losing the romance that she craved, Lola became despondent, fat and slovenly. Finally after he had used up all his inheritance in drinking, Doc joined Alcoholics Anonymous. His only hope for staying sober was never to think of the past—about what might have been. While Lola pined for what she had lost, Doc said: "We gotta keep on living, don't we? Let's not talk about it anymore. I gotta keep goin'—somehow."

Moderation Is the Answer

So we come to the answer to the question, "how much?" It has been implied in what has been said. It is again not a legal rule but a principle to apply. It is *moderation.*

But it is not moderation in terms of the love of one for the other. Love should have no limitations. It is moderation in the physical expression of that love—for love's sake. In other words the more love we have for each other the more we are moved to guide our activities as a couple in line with our best interests as a couple.

We can compare the difference in our use of the marks of affection in dating and in marriage with the difference in our use of an automobile in a congested city and in the open country.

When you drive a car down the main street of a large city, you regulate your speed so that you can control your car for frequent and sudden stops. You may chafe under the restrictions and wish to open the throttle to the full expression of the auto's speed, but you know the circumstances will not allow it. But when you are out in the open highway you can travel fifty to sixty miles per hour in comparative safety.

The acceleration of our feelings in courtship is like driving on Main Street. The acceleration in marriage compares to driving on the open highway. The difference in the situation determines the difference in operation. The nature of our relationship determines the way we regulate our affections. The analogy, of course, limps because the human being is not a machine. Yet the point remains that marriage is one thing and courtship is another. The responsibilities that go with marriage are quite another thing from the responsibilities that go with courtship—even in engagement.

What Is Moderation?

You may ask, "How do you know what is moderate?"

Perhaps I should spell it out in terms of specific regulations. I will do this to an extent in the chapter on wholesome dating. Yet "spelling it out" may miss the main point. Where there is a will to be moderate, moderation in all likelihood will result. But if we are not convinced in our inner self that moderation is what we want, all the minute regulations that could be devised would be of little avail. It is easy to rationalize our way around a rule when we have a mind to.

Moderation helps us to keep the various activities of our lives in their most constructive roles. Otherwise one of them may take on another role which is destructive. Somebody has said that any virtue pushed too far becomes a vice. Take eating, for example. In its proper role it is vital for our health and contributes to our enjoyment. When we become immoderate in our eating, the very food meant for health and enjoyment can become the means for undermining both.

As we apply this to the marks of affection, we see that used moderately they fulfill their constructive role as an expression of the courtship. Used immoderately they go beyond the role of an expression and become the *objective* of the courtship—the purpose for which it exists. When this happens they become destructive to the courtship.

As it is difficult to describe exactly where moderation ends and immoderation begins in the marks of affection, so also it is in eating. Yet if we have a mind to be moderate in eating at any particular meal, we know quite definitely how to go about it. So it is with the marks of affection. When we have the mind to be moderate, we have within us the indicators and awarenesses necessary to carry out our intentions.

Moderation in courtship is not easy. It is the result of honest-to-goodness effort. This is why the *desire* to be moderate has to come first. But where moderation seems beyond reach, it is usually because the overindulgence is making up for some other lack in a person's life. Some people tend to overeat when other basic needs—such as the need for love or for self-worth—are not being met. It is as though they were trying to oversatisfy one appetite to compensate for the undersatisfaction in others.

So also with the marks of affection. Harold, for example, felt defeated in his attempts to be moderate in his relationship with Beth. But after he had carefully looked into the problem he saw that he also had a family problem. His mother and father did not get along. They were arguing and fighting most of the time. As a result, whatever attention they were able to give to their children was cross and critical. Harold recalled leaving the house on more than one evening thoroughly fed up with the strife that was going on inside. It was at these times that moderation on his dates was most difficult.

Jessica had trouble with moderation too. She thought at the time it was because she was so much in love. It was not until after her romance came to an end that she saw another reason. Jessica was afraid of marriage because she had come from a broken home. She felt that any marriage of hers was doomed to the same end. Most of this was unclear to her at the time. But when her boy friend wanted to talk about the future—about getting married— Jessica instinctively tried to divert his attention through her physical affections. Here the threat of the future was drowned out by the emotional appeal of the present.

Moderation in courtship has two dimensions. The one pertains to the kind of activity—the limitations to sexual affection that go with courtship. The other pertains to the amount of the activity—the time factor. Feelings of affection are good. They need direction and control so that the effects also may be good. Moderation is a principle or a spirit that is needed for the best in living in all stages of life. Even marriage is not exempt. After encouraging married couples to follow their natural feelings in their love for each other, the noted marriage counselor Dr. H. W. Long says, "Only this, let all be in moderation. Carry nothing to excess."

It may help to point out that the Creator has designed man so that his sexual nature is aroused more quickly than a woman's. Of course there are exceptions. Yet it is good for a girl to know that her boy friend may be ahead of her in the acceleration of his feelings. On the other hand it is more difficult for the girl to know the state of her excitation since her sexual feelings are more diffuse than a boy's.

One thing she may know, however, is that her boy friend is probably more excited than she is. Once her feelings are fully aroused, this distinction no longer exists. This does not mean that the girl is more responsible than the boy for holding to the spirit of moderation. A Christian young man is as desirous as a Christian young woman to do the will of God. But it is a good thing for both to know that this difference exists. Little things a girl may do, which to her mean little—her dress, her touch, her talk—may be more strongly stimulating to her boy friend than she imagines.

Pregnancy and Disease

Perhaps you have noticed that in this whole discussion of sexual ethics I have not mentioned the dangers of pregnancy or of disease. I have purposely omitted these from the main body of the material because they are so often used to scare people into being moral. Frankly, I doubt whether this can be done successfully. Such scare tactics seem only to challenge us to a new order of "morality," namely, "Thou shalt not get caught."

With modern birth control and safety measures it is becoming easier not to get caught, though it may still happen—and does. It is very ironic that even with our birth control measures the number of unwed mothers is now statistically at an all-time high. The danger of disease is most acute when one has relations with a person who has been promiscuous.

Actually we have the same moral issue involved in premarital and extramarital relationships that result in pregnancy as in those that have been fortunate enough to avoid it. We have seen this from the Christian understanding of the meaning of the sexual relationship. The very idea that a baby might be conceived in such a union, however, adds an innocent person to the number who will be hurt by this action. Babies, like marriages, need all the favorable circumstances they can have as they enter life. Growing up is hard even in the best of families. Even when marriage does take place after the conception, the fact that this child was conceived out of wedlock can be an embarrassing situation for the parents and later on for the child. Nor can a boy really be motivated by love for his girl when he exposes her to this ordeal in our society.

Perhaps we can get an understanding of some of the possible complications that are involved if we look at it from the point of view of the future. Charles Collins did not know what was bothering him, but it had been bothering him for a long time, and he thought he had better get some help.

"I don't know what's wrong," he said, as soon as the small talk was over. "All I know is that I can get into such moods of despair that I don't know what to do with myself."

"Really black," I said.

"That's right. The worst part of it is that I'm going with an awfully nice girl. But whenever she brings up the subject of the future I get anxious inside and try to change the subject. I know this hurts her. And I don't want to make her unhappy. I don't know what the connection between my moods and my girl friend is, but I think there is one."

"The future isn't something you like to think about."

"No," he said. "So often I can't see any purpose in life.

When I feel this way I'd argue with anybody who said there *is* any purpose in living. This is when I'm really in black despair."

"I would imagine it is hard for you to believe in God when you feel this way," I said.

"I know it is and I hate that," he said. "When I'm in a better frame of mind I really do believe in God. In fact, if it were not for my religion, I'm sure I'd be worse off than I am."

"God has been of help to you then."

Charles did not answer. He was obviously thinking about something else—something emotionally disturbing. "I feel guilty," he said.

"About what?"

"About my folks. But don't ask me why, because I can't pin it down to anything. I feel sorry for them. I want to do something to help them, but I don't know what or how."

"You evidently feel they need help."

"Well, they've had it hard," he said. "They've both had to work hard to raise us kids." Charles clenched his teeth. "There I get that guilty feeling again."

"You mean when you mentioned about your parents' having to work hard to raise the family?"

"Yes—something just flip-flops inside of me whenever I think about this."

"Does it bring up painful memories?"

Charles did not answer, but I had a feeling he would, and so I kept quiet. "They used to fight a lot—lots more than they do now," he said finally. "I can remember how frightened I would get when in the midst of their fighting they would threaten to leave each other. But then—then they always ended up by saying they had to stick it out because of the children."

"How did this make you feel?"

"Like it was I who was keeping them from doing what they wanted to. I felt guilty—that's it—guilty."

"You evidently felt more responsible than the other children."

"Well, I'm the oldest and—"

"Yes?"

"Well—Mom and Dad *had* to get married if you know what I mean."

"In other words you feel more responsible because you were the one who brought them together in the first place."

"That's right," he said. "I know it isn't sensible to feel this way, but I do. I used to more than I do now. In other families wedding anniversaries and birthdays are times of happiness. But in our home it's always been uncomfortable at these times. You know why."

"Because of the closeness of the anniversary to your birthday?"

"Yes—I think it bothered Mom more than it did Dad. It was always embarrassing for her when people asked her how old I was—or when somebody would ask her how long she and Dad had been married. You could always count on her being in a mood for a couple of days afterward."

"All of this didn't help your mood either, did it?"

"No—I can see it better now, and also why I feel the way I do about getting married myself. I wouldn't want a marriage like my folks have. But I don't suppose my marriage would *have* to be unhappy—would it?"

Marks of Affection Belong

The marks of affection have their place in a wholesome courtship. It is not that they are merely tolerated; they belong there. But if their use is intensified to the type of love-making that pertains to the marital relationship, their influence can become destructive rather than helpful. Keeping our expressions of affection within the limitations of our relationship promotes the greatest welfare of all concerned.

The sexual relationship of marriage is a developing experience. From its beginning it needs the advantage of a free atmosphere both within and without. The development of the marital union of body, mind and spirit can use all the favorable advantages that a wholesome courtship can offer. You can begin now to make the most out of your marriage in the future by making the most out of your dating and courtship.

5

The Wisdom
of the Christian
Structure of Life

One writer in the field of sex says, "Young people, being human, would like a simple yes or no, to which they might conform or against which they might rebel."

If this is true, we need to aim for something beyond conformity or rebellion, namely, conviction. When we are sold on something, it is because we have seen the wisdom of it—that it makes sense. So it is our purpose in this chapter to show both the wisdom of having a structure to life and the particular wisdom behind the Christian structure.

Rebellion Against Restraint

Why is it that young people want a yes or no in order that they may conform or rebel? Is it not because they have thought of rules and regulations in terms of restraints, and restraints in terms of parents or others in authority?

If you identify yourself with these authorities then you conform. If you are in rebellion against them you resist, either outwardly or inwardly. When you rebel it is because you suspect your parents or others—and these others usually include God—are trying to run your life. You resist this interference because you want to run your own life.

Rebellion may be a desperate attempt to remain free. All who are in authority are constantly tempted to abuse that authority. The Bible warns against this very thing when it warns against overcorrection. Overcorrection is an evil as well as undercorrection. Christian teaching and Christian discipline are something other than either. Overcorrection may cause us to conform so that we may be accepted by our parents and others in authority.

The Creator's "Rules" Are Different

Unfortunately God is often blocked out by these attitudes we have toward human authorities. In reality the very thing that distorts our attitude toward discipline does not exist in the Creator's "rules." His structure to life is the way to real freedom.

God designed life according to an intelligent plan. The human personality is no exception. In fact it is the crowning achievement of God's designing. We are created in God's own image. This means He designed us to function with Himself as our center—with Himself as our object of worship. Trouble comes when we get off-centered, that is, when we worship something less than God. By worship I mean that we give to something less than God the importance and devotion that belong only to God. This is

what the Bible calls *sin*—"worshipping and serving the *creature* [that which is created] rather than the Creator."

How do you react to this word *sin?* It has become something of an offensive word in our society. Maybe we have used it too often to frighten people, particularly children. Perhaps it frightens you. Let us try to take an objective look at it so we can understand what it is all about. We could banish the word *sin* but this would not banish what the word stands for. We live in a world in which there are moral values and moral choices. We can speak of something being right only in contrast to what is wrong. We can talk about the good only as the opposite of the evil. The fact that I can make the wrong choice morally is simply another way of saying that I can sin. The fact that everyone makes wrong as well as right moral decisions is another way of saying that sin is universal. Nor is it simply a matter of being ignorant. I can know what is right and still do the wrong. It is a result of our freedom.

If sin has its origin in worshiping something less than God, what is this rival to God for our devotion? The answer is I, myself. We pit our wills against His will. We have the tendency to want to be our own god.

When Margaret Slater talked about her problem she gave an example of how this tendency works. She was just two months short of being eighteen years old. I had heard that she had been going out with a man who was twelve years older than she. The problem was that he had a wife and two children. I met her unexpectedly one day as I was doing some errands. She seemed to be uncomfortable in making conversation, and so I was not surprised when she said, "Well, I suppose you've been hearing things about me."

"As a matter of fact, I have," I said.

"I certainly never thought it would happen to me," she said. "I certainly didn't plan it this way. Nor did Joe. It just happened."

"You mean you don't feel responsible for what's happened," I said.

"I met him one day at a friend's house," she said. "It was raining and so he took me home. We just became good friends. We found we could talk to each other so well. Well—one day we discovered we loved each other. I know what we are doing is supposed to be wrong. But the way we feel about each other—it just can't be wrong."

"You think this makes it right."

"I don't see how it can be wrong," she said earnestly. "My whole life has meaning now. I realize that I'd never known what real happiness was until I met Joe. He's so different from the fellows I ran around with. He's so much more mature and polished."

"Dating him is different from dating fellows your own age," I said.

"Oh—there's no comparison! They seem to be just little boys. I never knew what a real man was like until I met Joe. He feels that I'm for him, too. His wife just doesn't understand him. He says he's never known real love until he met me. I know I've helped him too. He used to drink too much. He doesn't any more. But he says if I quit seeing him, he knows he'll go back to it. His wife just isn't nice to him. So you see—it just *has* to be right!"

"You want very much to believe it is right," I said.

"I feel it's nobody's business but our own," she said with an expression of defiance. "I don't believe I have to conform to other people's opinions. They're just a bunch of nosy gossips anyhow. They're doing things a lot worse, and nobody says anything!"

"What about God's opinion?" I asked.

Margaret swallowed hard. "I can't see where it's wrong," she said. "The way we love each other—I just can't give him up. I do feel sorry for his children. But as Joe says—it is just as well to be brought up in a broken home than in a home where there's no love. I don't think his wife has any right to him—the way she treats him! I can make him happy."

"I see."

"Maybe I'm being selfish—but I still don't want to give him up. Why did we ever meet—if I was to give him up?"

"You feel God had something to do with your meeting him."

"It doesn't seem fair," she said. "What will my life be now—without him!" Margaret was close to tears. The real issue was now out in the open. It was hard to face.

If we examine Margaret's problem we can see that she was trying to escape responsibility for her actions by implying that something beyond her control was responsible. "I didn't plan it. It just happened. Why did we meet at all—if I was to give him up?" It is always tempting to avoid the responsibility for our moral choices by adopting a fatalistic attitude. "I can't help it—I'm the victim of circumstances." The fact that Margaret could at any time make the moral decision to stop seeing Joe makes her decision to continue seeing him a voluntary one—for which she has a responsibility.

We notice also that she was trying to justify her actions on the basis of her feelings. Since they loved each other, their actions had to be right. She was resentful of any "higher" law that contradicted her feelings that she was right. Such a law "was not fair." Actually she was a law unto herself. She tried for awhile to justify this "law" by blaming the wife's behavior and by pointing out how much Joe needed her, but she finally brought out quite clearly that her "law" was for *her* sake. Here is the self-center (the *I*) pitting itself against any higher devotion (God)—demanding what it wants regardless of whom or what may stand in the way.

Sin is more than simply breaking the rules. It centers in an attitude. I exalt myself over against God, and for that matter, against my fellow human beings as well. When I do this I am actually sinning against my own nature as a human being. In fact somebody has defined sin as our unwillingness to accept ourselves as human beings. We either want to be something more than a human being—a god, or something less than a human being—a lower animal with no responsibility for his actions.

If sin centers in an attitude, where do rules or commandments come in? They are needed as signposts to mark out the differences in major life situations between an attitude that is self-centered and one that is God-centered. We need these signposts because of our predisposition to become confused by our emotions. Margaret wanted to believe that because of the way she and Joe felt about each other, their relationship could not be wrong. Something that stands out clearly through the fog of such feelings—something like "Thou shalt not covet thy neighbor's spouse," or something about the sanctity of marriage and the home—is necessary for our guidance.

Moral laws such as the Ten Commandments outline a structure to our living. If we go counter to this structure, we go counter to our basic nature as designed in God's image. The result is obviously negative. It hurts to kick against the pricks. It is like going against the grain. As somebody has said, "We don't break the Ten Commandments; the Commandments break us." Sin throws a monkey wrench into our living. Even as selfishness creates chaos within us in terms of envy and resentment, so it creates chaos in our living with others in terms of strife and deceit.

If sin centers in an attitude, its opposite must also center in an attitude. What is its opposite? The answer again lies in our true nature—the divine image. God is love. If we are created in His image, we fulfill our nature by loving. Love is the opposite of sin. The pattern of life that God has revealed to us in His law is a description of how love operates. This is why St. Paul can say, "He who loves his neighbor has fulfilled the law. The commandments, 'You shall not commit adultery, You shall not kill, You shall not steal, You shall not covet,' and any other commandments, are summed up in this sentence, 'You shall love your neighbor as yourself.' " [1]

Help from the Greeks

The word love covers a lot. We can see this from Margaret's experience. It has become a catch-all for everything from heroic sacrifice to outright selfishness. Actually the meaning of love has too many sides to be described by just one word.

The Greek language in which the New Testament was first written has three words for love. It is unfortunate that the English language does not offer a similar selection so that more accurate translations could be made. The first of these two Greek words is *eros*. This is romantic love. The second is *philia*. This is the love we find in close friendships. The third is *agape*. *Agape* goes beyond the natural attractions of romance or friendship, and is mo-

[1] Romans 13:8-9

tivated by the *will* to love—not only certain people but all people, not only the likable but also the unlikable. We see this love most clearly in the love of Christ.

Naturally *eros* is very important to the relationships of courtship and marriage. Being romantic in character, *eros* centers in the physical expression of affection. It is the God-given quality that makes the love of lovers different from that of friends. Yet *eros* was not made to exist by itself. It needs the company of *philia* and *agape* or it may cease to be love at all.

Here is where we meet a problem. During the relationships of dating and courtship *eros* tends to want to go it alone. Lovers who experience its presence are inclined to make it the only guide for their decisions and actions. This is particularly true when the people involved have been deprived of emotional evidences of affection in their earlier life. It is hard for the hungry person not to overeat when he has the opportunity for food.

Romantic Love Is Not Enough

Decisions based on *eros* alone are likely to be decisions based on the desires and emotions of the moment. This is why we have a vow in the wedding ceremony. Why should two people who are much in love have to promise to love each other? For the simple reason that *eros* has a way of ebbing and flowing. Therefore something more than the present desire is needed to form a marriage to last a lifetime.

That something more is the will to love when one does not feel like it. That is *agape*. It works through *eros* and it works outside of it. Marriage cannot be based only on what we call the romantic atmosphere. This comes and goes in marriage. It is *agape* that enables one to take the other for better or for worse. It is *agape* in love that makes it the fulfillment of God's law.

Eros also needs *philia*. The things in common that bind together good friends are needed for marital partners because marital partners among other things need to be good friends. It is these mutual interests and concerns which deepen the love of husband and wife through the years and in this way deepen also the expression of *eros* in their marriage. Without *philia, eros* tends to dry up and disappear in the day-by-day living of married life. Because it is an essentially romantic love, *eros* is dependent upon novelty, atmosphere, and adventure. While these qualities can continue in marriage, there are times when they are noticeably absent. Married life is also made up of the unromantic—routine, sameness, unimaginative living, taking each other for granted, absorption in making a living. Naturally these elements pose a problem for *eros*. There is even a book entitled *How to Keep Romance in Your Marriage*.

Eros is a sensitive love. It cannot *take* much. Fear can temporarily squelch it. So can resentment. After you live with a person you begin to react to his bodily appearance as you do to his personality. If you have a grievance toward the person, he becomes less attractive to you physically. So it is in marriage. When this happens old attractions can settle into mutual indifference.

Much can be done to avoid this danger to *eros* in marriage. Much can also be done to restore *eros*. Thoughtfulness will go a long way to help. So will showing understanding. Planned activities are another essential. But it is the *philia* and *agape* qualities of married love that hold the ties when *eros* is down, so that *eros* can rise again. The will to work at maintaining or restoring the romantic quality to marriage comes from the loyalty to each other that is inherent in these other qualities.

So it is clear that in courtship the *eros* which is normally the dominant attraction needs to be examined in the light of *philia* and *agape* before any plans for the future can be dependable. Activities in our dating that reveal and develop *philia* and disciplinary measures that call forth *agape* are excellent experiences for courtship because they are excellent preparations for marriage. In this manner the decisions we make will be guided not only by the immediate desires of *eros* but also by the more rational qualities of *philia* and *agape*. They will be decisions for the best interests of all concerned both in the present and in the future.

Why a Marriage Ceremony?

Love provides its own structure for our relationships in dating and courtship. Yet we need to guard against the rationalizations that come about through the tendency of *eros* to go it alone.

Bob and Connie believed they really loved each other and planned to marry. But for practical reasons they thought it wise to postpone marriage until Bob finished another year of college. While they accepted this postponement intellectually, emotionally they rebelled against it. When Bob came to see me he was trying to resolve this conflict.

"We're having a problem of petting," he said. "I feel guilty about it—and yet, I can't convince myself there's anything wrong with it. Isn't it all convention anyhow—this idea of getting married. Does that little wedding ceremony make that much difference? Isn't it sort of odd that we are always supposed to be holding our feelings down until a certain ceremony takes place, and then all of a sudden we have to reverse ourselves and let our feelings go? I won't love Connie any more on the day we are married than I do now. Seems to me that the most important thing is being married in the eyes of God. Why should we be frustrated because of society's rules?"

"When do you think marriage takes place in the eyes of God?" I asked.

"When two people profess their love for each other," he said.

"Then why not get married in the eyes of the State?" I asked.

"Because it isn't practical just now."

"You mean, you aren't ready to accept the full responsibility of what marriage means in the eyes of the State?" I asked.

Bob saw what I was getting at but he was not in any mood to yield a point.

"Sure, I know we have got to have law and order," he said. "I wouldn't recommend what I'm saying for general practice. But for Connie and me it seems different."

As soon as Bob said this he grinned a little sheepishly. What he wanted for himself he could not advocate for others.

If we are not ready to assume the responsibilities of marriage in the eyes of the State, we can scarcely be ready in the eyes of God, for God's expectations of marriage are surely not less than those of the State. God is not opposed to the government of the State as Bob implied. Orderly government is necessary for human welfare. This is why Bob would not advocate his ideas for all to follow. God works through the State as well as through the Church. For this reason a Christian respects the laws of the land.

It helped Bob to talk it out. He saw more clearly the wisdom of orderly procedure and the rationalizing role his own emotions were playing. One can not have his cake and eat it too. For love's sake the sexual union is kept within the context of the marital union, and marriage is kept within the context of the order of the State.

Guilt—Good or Bad?

Perhaps the conclusions to which we have come so far in this book have aroused in you a sense of guilt. Perhaps you feel uncomfortable and uneasy about this whole subject. As we all know, guilt is a miserable feeling. It is the tension we experience over the contrast between what we are and what we believe we should be. Despite its unpleasantness, its whole purpose in God's design is to encourage a change for the better. If we never felt any dissatisfaction with ourselves, we would probably never experience much improvement either.

But guilt can also be bad for us. It is bad when there is no solution to it—when all it does is defeat and depress us. When this happens our guilt causes us to do worse rather than better.

Because she could find no hope in her guilt, Joyce had reached a state where she was chronically upset. It was very hard for her to get up enough courage to come to me. And when she arrived it was even more difficult for her to express her problem. I could see that she really had something she wanted to say and so I gave her plenty of time.

"I'm afraid something is going to happen to me," she said haltingly.

"What particularly?" I asked.

"I don't know for sure," she said.

"Have you any clues?"

"Well—just this—I keep remembering my grandmother telling me never to do bad things or to tempt the Lord because He would punish me."

"When was this, Joyce?"

"When I was just a little girl," she said. "I had been with some neighbor kids. We were—were playing with ourselves—you know, exploring with sex. And we got caught. I got an awful spanking. I'll never forget it."

"Can you remember your feelings at the time?" I asked.

"I didn't understand too much except that we must have been doing something awfully bad. I guess I thought *I* was bad."

"And did that stop the sex play?"

"No—we just made sure nobody ever caught us again."

"And what does all this have to do with your present fears?" I asked.

"I'm about as low as you can get," she said. "I've gotten myself a reputation. I don't think any decent boy would go with me. I'm not good enough for any decent boy."

"I see you haven't got a very high opinion of yourself."

"I'm no good," she said. "I feel like such a hypocrite when I come to Church. Whenever I try to read the Bible, it seems to be full of condemnation."

"You feel God is going to punish you for the things you are doing."

"I try not to think of it, but the harder I try, the more these fears go through my mind—and the more I go on doing the things I know I shouldn't."

"It's a vicious cycle, isn't it? The more guilty you feel, the more unforgivable you feel you are. And the more unforgivable you feel you are, the more you go on doing the things you know you should not."

"I don't feel good enough to come to God," she said.

Then with anguish in her voice, "Oh, why does there have to be such a thing as sex anyhow?"

"You feel angry toward God for creating it."

"Now that I have the reputation I have, it's awfully hard to get out of it. Fellows seem to date me for only one reason." Joyce looked somewhat bitter as she said this. "I've never told anybody these things before, and it was awfully hard doing it this time."

Joyce had taken the first step in turning her guilt from a destructive power into a power for good. It helps to talk these problems of guilt over with a clergyman.

God does not want religion to be a power for condemnation, but a power for overcoming. To help people in realizing this power the Church has its office of the ministry.

Joyce's guilt was not what God intended. As Christians we know that He is a forgiving God. We have in the Cross of Jesus God's own assurance of forgiveness to all who really desire it. When you let Him forgive you as He wants to do, you feel close to Him again. There is a healing power in the experience of forgiveness which can even eliminate in the course of time some of the bad consequences of our ways. Of equal importance is the experience of oneness with God that we have through forgiveness. It supplies us with the power to do better.

Because she did not want to lose him, Patsy in a moment of emotional excitation gave in to her boy friend's desires. In the days that followed she felt very guilty about the whole thing. It worried her that he would want to do the same thing again. She decided to go to her pastor.

After she had told him everything she expressed her fears that the matter was not over. She loved her boy friend and wanted to think he loved her. But she was afraid that he would become insistent again and might leave her if she refused. Through the help of the pastor she was led to an experience of forgiveness and to the courage to remain firm in her convictions regardless of the cost.

Her fears were well grounded. On the next date her boy friend forced the issue. She told him how she felt. He admitted that he believed in God and wanted to do what God wants, except in this one case. She told him she could never again go along with this. The result was also what she feared. He began to date somebody else.

Later she told her pastor: "I think he will still take me out or I will know that he really didn't love me very much and was taking me out to see what he could get from me. After I got home from my date, I really felt good and had a peace about me. I got down on my knees and thanked God for giving me the courage and strength for doing what I did."

Four Qualities of Character

The qualities of character needed for a wholesome courtship are the same qualities that are needed for a wholesome marriage. The first of these is *honesty*.

We need people who are the same on the inside as they are on the outside. There is nothing so disruptive to any human relationship as distrust. In counseling with married couples who are having trouble, I find my greatest difficulty in those cases where the sincerity of one of the partners is in doubt. Being honest in our intentions is fundamental to any genuine getting along with others.

The second quality is *wisdom*. The best way to describe wisdom is to describe what it is not. We have a good example of this in the person of Esau in the Old Testament.[2] As the oldest son he had inherited the birthright, which in this case meant the promise that through his family God would bless all nations. One day when Esau returned from his hunting, he found his brother Jacob cooking food. The smell of the food was too much for him. "Let me eat some of that red pottage, for I am famished," he said.

Jacob saw his advantage. "First sell me your birthright," he said.

Esau did not even deliberate. "I am about to die; of what use is a birthright to me?" So he sold it for a mess of pottage.

Later Esau himself realized that he had made an unwise trade. But at the moment all he cared about was the satisfaction of his hunger. He failed to recognize the lasting values.

We have seen how wisdom is necessary in making the decisions that go with dating and courtship, particularly concerning the physical expression of affection. How much more will this same wisdom be needed in the many complicated problems that arise in marriage and family living?

The third quality is *strength*. The action of Esau may have been due to weakness as much as to a lack of wisdom. Some persons recognize values at least intellectually but seem unable to carry through on these values when pressed by more immediate desires.

Under the stress of losing her boy friend, Patsy was tempted to make an unwise decision. Yet she was able to hold to her convictions. This took strength of character.

There are young people who comfort themselves for their lack of strength in dating by looking forward to mar-

[2] Genesis 25:29-34

riage as a cure-all, in which no more sexual limitations will be needed. The truth is that there are times of privation in marriage also. Pregnancy, particularly during the latter weeks, is one of those times. After the baby is born is another. Periods of physical and emotional stress or forced absences are others. Will the person who was too weak to discipline his impulses before marriage suddenly find the strength to do so after marriage?

The fourth quality is *love*. Love, of course, is a governing factor in honesty, wisdom, and strength. Yet it is something more than these.

To seek the welfare of the other may make it necessary at times to put aside our own needs and desires—to give without demanding a return. To rise to this stature is not only the mark of maturity; it is the mark of love. "Love suffers long and is kind; love is not jealous or boastful; it is not arrogant or rude. Love does not insist on its own way; it is not irritable or resentful; it does not rejoice at wrong, but rejoices in the right. Love bears all things, believes all things, hopes all things, endures all things. Love never ends." [3]

Here is the foundation for dating and courtship because it is the foundation of marriage.

[3] I Corinthians 13:4-8

6

Sex in Solitude

"Ninety-nine out of a hundred teenage boys and girls masturbate—and the other one's a liar." So says a recent book on teenagers. You may say, "I don't and I'm not a liar!" Or you may say, "I guess I have a lot of company."

The statement is admittedly an exaggeration. It comes from youth counselors who have to deal with this problem so often that they conclude it is universal. But it is not. There are young people who do not masturbate. There are also many who do. Even though we lack reliable statistics, it is obvious that masturbation is a problem, and that any book on the Christian view of sex needs to discuss it.

What Is It?

What is masturbation? The word comes from the Latin, *masturbari*, which means to defile oneself by one's hands. We also call it autostimulation, which means self-stimulation. It is the practice of bringing about a release of sexual tension—or orgasm—by rubbing the genital area. Some young people discover this possibility more or less accidentally. Others are introduced to it by older youths. Still others may have little or no experience with it.

Is it a good thing to do? Or a bad thing to do? Or does it make any difference? Perhaps some of you have heard some rather weird things about what may happen to you if you do—things like losing your mind or harming yourself physically. Some people actually believe these things. But mostly these are stories to scare youngsters out of masturbating. So far as having any basis in fact, they are merely superstitions.

This is not to say that masturbation has no consequences. Every act has its consequences. But before we take up the consequences we need to evaluate the cause. If sexual tension as a physiological process were the only force behind the need to masturbate, the problem would not be so complicated. But it is not. Masturbation as an occasional exploratory venture on the part of the teenager is one thing; masturbation as a compulsive and regular release from emotional tensions is another.

Substitute for a Solution

We have seen that God created men and women as sexual beings that they might relate one to another in a union of love. When we have difficulties as young people in our relationships with others—when we have trouble getting along with Mother and Dad and the kids at school —our sexual nature is affected. We all need emotionally satisfying relationships with others for our happiness and wholesome development. When these are lacking, our entire inner life becomes disturbed. One of the outcomes may be an increase in sexual tension. This is simply nature's way of trying to heal the breach. It is an expression of the desire for union with another and a protest against emotional and spiritual isolation.

If we try to satisfy this increased tension by masturbation, we end up disappointed. For despite the physical release that masturbation may bring, we remain alone. The danger is that because masturbation does offer some sort of an immediate release to this sexual tension, it may become a substitute for the real thing—for wholesome personal relationships. When this happens it becomes an escape from reality. Like alcohol, when used as an escape masturbation becomes more and more needed and more and more of a habit. Because the need for social experience is partially even if illusorily met by masturbation, there is less drive left to do something about the real problem. While we can see that compulsive masturbation of this nature is a symptom of emotional disturbance, it also adds to the problem by substituting for the solution.

The Problem of Guilt

It adds to the problem also in another manner. Masturbation has a way of making people feel guilty. I have counseled with young people who for all practical purposes felt that their addiction to masturbation disqualified them from the love of God—a type of unforgivable sin.

There are reasons for this. In the first place, we have tended in our religious circles to place a heavier censorship on the "sins of the body" than on the "sins of the spirit." Secondly, and perhaps because of this, masturbation is a hard thing to talk about. You may feel ashamed to bring this problem to your parents or your pastor or even your school counselors. Keeping something locked up inside of us because of shame increases the shame.

In the third place masturbation itself is usually done in

secret. Nobody shares the experience with you. You take precautions to avoid discovery. All of this increases the guilt.

Finally, there are the thoughts that may accompany the anticipation of the masturbation experience. We compensate for our aloneness by concocting an erotic atmosphere in our minds. We imagine the presence of another, and work in all sorts of sexual fantasies. Of course this makes the atmosphere all the more misleading. When the experience is over, not only are we more alone than before, but we can no longer justify to ourselves the thoughts which we had. It does not seem as though we are even the same person. Because of these changes in us, we have a hard time accepting ourselves.

Some writers on this subject feel that the guilt about masturbation is the greatest danger in masturbation. They say this not only because guilt is painful, but because it may cause a person to become even more withdrawn than he already is. We have seen that addiction to masturbation may be a symptom of difficulty in relating to others. If the symptom is followed by a sense of shame and worthlessness, the person feels even less qualified to associate with others. As a result he withdraws even more into himself, and becomes more addicted to his habit.

Naturally, religion gets a bad name in all of this because it is the so-called religious conscience that is credited with causing the guilt. Unfortunately, in our culture religion and Christianity are too often thought of as synonymous. Actually Christianity centers in the solution of guilt, not in the fixation of it. Whenever we see guilt pile up and become destructive in its influence, we see a person who is in need of the good news of Christianity, not one who has it.

In spite of all this, the guilt about masturbation has a basis in fact. The real longing has not been met, even though the buildup in anticipation seems to indicate that it will be. The sexual fantasies appear afterward to be foolish if not revolting. We feel let down. A mere physical sensation cannot bring the satisfactions of joining with another, any more than fantasy can take the place of reality. What follows is a sense of being cheated, or even worse, of having cheated oneself.

Coming to a Decision

To answer the question whether masturbation serves our best interests, we need to submit it to the total meaning of love for self. Love for self is not something to apologize for, but something to work for. God thought enough of love for self to make it the pattern for love to others. "Thou shalt love thy neighbor as thyself." Love for self is often mistaken for selfishness. Actually selfishness is something quite different. It is a perversion of love for self. In the name of looking out for himself first, last, and always, the selfish person appears to be seeking his own best interests, but his attitude toward himself and toward others is so basically negative that all he does is bring about his own misery.

It is amazing how much of human behavior is self-destructive. Take for instance how some people flirt with death in the way they handle their automobiles. Others slowly but surely destroy their mental and physical health by overindulgence in alcohol. Then there is the whole area of emotionally induced physical illness. Physicians estimate that from thirty to fifty per cent of their patients are making themselves physically ill by harboring destructive feelings deep within them. Even nail biting is an example.

Though it is a habit and difficult to overcome, it is obviously destructive in producing needless pain and in what it does to the appearance of our hands. Nor have we yet mentioned the misery brought on by our self-induced worries and grievances, our need to suffer and fret, and the general emotional chaos which we insist on provoking.

Even animals know better. Most of them instinctively take good care of themselves. But instinct and freedom are two different things. Because we have the power of choice, we can knowingly do the harmful. We can realize we are hurting ourselves by what we are doing, and still keep doing it. Sometimes we hear people justify this unconscious tendency toward suicide by saying, "I know it's not good for me, but after all, I'm not hurting anybody but myself."

Such a statement shows how little appreciation we can have of our own worth—how little we may actually like ourselves. Behind it all there is probably a deep-seated rejection of ourselves—perhaps even a hatred for ourselves. If we look at the end results, selfishness may actually come closer to a hatred for the self than to a love for the self. It always leads to an impoverishment of the spirit.

Here we get an insight into an essential characteristic of love. Certainly a person may have plenty of reason to reject himself. But love is forgiving—accepting even the unacceptable. Love recognizes the worth and value of the human personality in spite of its shortcomings. Love is interested in the potential for wholesome development within every person as he lives his life under God. "Every person" includes ourselves. Loving ourselves is not a matter of being selfish in our decisions but of being interested in our development as persons. So also in our dealings with our neighbor—be it man or woman, boy or girl—we are guided by our interest in his or her wholesome development. This is what it means to love him as ourself.

What do we see when we submit masturbation to the judgment of the total meaning of love for self? There is obviously the satisfaction of a release from sexual tension. There is also the fact that sexual experience has been adapted to isolated activity. If this becomes a habit we may find it difficult to adapt this sexual experience to an object other than ourselves, namely to the mate of our choice. The problem is not so much the physical adaptation—although this too could be a problem—but the whole attitude toward the experience. In other words when we turn inward upon ourselves that experience meant to turn us outward toward another, we may not find it natural to reverse the process in our attitudes when the time comes. From this point of view masturbation may be closer to selfishness than to love for self.

The more our attitude toward ourselves is one of love, the more we can go beyond immediate tensions to see the issue in its totality, that is, to see it more or less objectively. From this point of view, love for self and discipline of self go together.

As we have seen, disciplining sexual desires in line with the best interests of all concerned is needed for dating and for marriage. Such discipline begins in our solitude. If we indulge our immediate impulses here, we may find it harder to maintain our discipline when it concerns others as well as ourselves. From my experience I have noticed that people who have indulged themselves in masturbation have corresponding trouble with temptation in dating. Our discipline so far as masturbation is concerned should not begin with the physical tensions but with the thoughts that encourage the tensions.

Resources for Discipline

Where are the resources for such discipline to be found? Boys have more difficulty with masturbation than girls. As boys reach puberty their bodies begin manufacturing semen. This is the substance that contains the male sperm cells used for reproduction. Because it is constantly being manufactured the semen needs an outlet. Pressure for such an outlet may manifest itself as sexual tension.

But this does not mean that something has to be done by the boy to relieve this pressure. The Creator has planned a system for its release. It is known as the night loss. During sleep the semen is ejected. By designing this involuntary method for release, God has made it unnecessary for the boy to resort to self-stimulation. He has a resource for discipline within his own natural functions.

These night losses are also referred to as "wet dreams." They may constitute a problem for some. The release of semen is often accompanied in sleep by a dream which is erotic in nature. A boy may be dismayed that he has such dreams. They may be out of keeping with his accepted standards.

It is unwise to take the imagery of dreams at its face value. What is being symbolized by the dream is simply the expression of this periodic physical and psychological pressure and its release. Beneath it all there is the deep and emotional desire to unite with another, for which sex is a medium.

It is not coincidence that we have our greatest difficulty with discipline in regard to masturbation during those times when we feel lonely or down in spirits. We want things to be different. So fantasy and masturbation may compensate for a void in our social and recreational life. Discipline in this case would not allow us to settle for compensations. Instead we will recognize the deeper nature of our needs and attempt to find an answer in terms of more creative activity and social experience. In doing so we are showing genuine love to our self.

But to find this creative and social outlet may seem too big a job for us. Perhaps you feel overcome by the problem in spite of what we have been saying. In this case you probably need person-to-person help. Go to a counselor— your parents, your pastor, your school counselor—and talk things over. The hold your problem has over you may be a symptom that deeper personality needs are not being met. Your first need is for a capable confidant with whom you can share your problem. This would be the beginning of developing more social contacts and emotionally satisfying relationships. When we need help it is a mark of strength for us to admit it, and a mark of courage to ask for it.

Because it is highly emotional in nature, the sex urge may be stronger than the powers of our reason to control. This is usually the case when it is being fed by underground streams, so that it is serving more purposes than it normally should. If these other purposes can be met in more wholesome ways, the pressure upon the sex drive will naturally lessen.

One major difference between the human being and the lower animals is that the human being has the potential for freedom, while the animal is largely controlled by his biological instinctive urges. The human being may have freedom even in regard to these urges. To fulfill this potential he needs to understand what is going on between his mind and his body. He also needs conviction and faith.

Dan had found these things out from experience. His last visit with me was primarily to relate his progress.

"I've been getting along real well," he said. "I think I'm over the hump."

"Tell me about it," I said.

"It helped me a lot to talk it out," he said. "I wasn't so afraid of my problem after that. I could understand things better. I could see more clearly why I was masturbating."

"Before this it was all somewhat of a mystery to you."

"I guess I thought of masturbation as the unforgivable sin—or something like that. I honestly thought if I could overcome it, I'd be just about perfect."

"It all focused there."

"Yeah—it kind of distorts your whole view of life," he said. "But it really feels good to be able to control myself."

"It helps your morale," I said.

"You said it. I was a slave to the habit—it was a crutch of the first water. I always told myself I should stop it— but even then I half knew I didn't mean it."

"You were kidding yourself."

"That's the real trouble right there," he said. "I'd always rationalize by saying, 'just this once more,' or 'once more won't hurt anything.'"

"It's hard to be determined when you are divided within yourself."

"That's why I came to the conclusion that if I was going to get control over it I couldn't masturbate at all," Dan said. "I understand that's the way with an alcoholic too. Since he's overdone drinking, he has to quit drinking altogether, or he won't quit being an alcoholic."

"Yes—that's the position of the Alcoholics Anonymous group."

"I realized through our talks that masturbation wasn't my real problem. Yet I had to do something about it directly because it was uppermost on my mind."

"You had to take yourself where you were," I said.

"Yes. And that meant I had to make a decision—and mean it."

"What do you feel helped you to do this?"

Dan hesitated before he answered. "This probably sounds trite," he said, "but I think God did. After you helped me see that I was forgiven, I felt that if I was sincere at all about this thing, I had to make up my mind."

"And then what happened?"

"I think this decision was the big thing," he said. "I had to mean business. Sure, I still slip once in a while, but I'm gaining ground and I know it."

"You don't evidently get as depressed afterward as you used to."

"No. I feel badly, of course. But it's different now. I don't feel condemned—I feel forgiven. I know God will help me if I really want help."

"And you believe you have been already receiving this help."

"Right," he said. "These sessions have helped out a whole lot. As I began to understand why I would masturbate, I was able to head it off better."

"Outsmart it?"

"Yeah. I know when I'm most likely to want to masturbate, and so I take precautions."

"How?"

"For one thing, when I start getting teed off, instead of doing as I used to do—keeping it to myself and getting disgusted and feeling sorry for myself—I get by myself and tell God about it. Sometimes it isn't a very nice prayer, but I know He understands. I feel a lot better afterward."

"Good emotional hygiene."

"I suppose you could call it that," Dan said. "I find too that praying at night helps. I try to keep praying until I go to sleep."

"Is this going to sleep saying your prayers?"

"It doesn't take long," he said with a grin. "I found a good prayer in some book. I try to say it as soon as I wake up in the morning. It goes like this:

O God, grant me strength to change the things that need to be changed, and courage to accept the things that cannot be changed, and the wisdom to know the difference."

"Yes, I've heard that prayer."

"Well—guess that's about it," he said. "I want to thank you for the help. I think I can get along o.k. now. I have some confidence in myself. Or maybe I should say I have some faith in God."

7

Sexual Abnormalities

I imagine you have read stories in the newspaper about people who are called sex perverts or sex deviates or some such name. Maybe you have heard your parents or the kids at school talk about them. There are many kinds of sexual abnormalities.

There are also many perverted ideas of what constitutes sexual perversion. Perhaps you have heard somebody referred to as a "fairy" simply because he is different from the gang. Even though you may not be sure of what it means, you view this person with suspicion. He is the victim of a label. If he needs any help, this attitude of others makes it harder than ever for him to get it. Therefore it is for our own benefit, as well as for those with whom we come in contact, that we have some idea of what is involved in sexual abnormalities.

Normal and Abnormal

First of all, what is a sexual abnormality? We can begin our definition by saying that it is behavior in the area of sex that is out of harmony with a person's stage in development.

Children are naturally curious about their bodies. They like to play doctor or nurse in an effort to satisfy this curiosity. They may even want to do it behind closed doors because they have a feeling that their elders would disapprove. I remember the day I got a phone call from a neighbor saying that our children and their children were playing Adam and Eve in their front yard. When I arrived they had doffed all their clothing and were parading around the front yard naked.

While it is a little disconcerting to adults, this behavior is entirely natural for children. They are curious about themselves and they are sexual beings even as children. The only unfortunate thing is that some adults may consider this behavior from an adult point of view and scold the children so hard that they feel guilty about the fact that God created them as sexual beings.

But now let us shift to another stage. A few years ago I attended a convention of young people on the campus of a large university. As I was walking to one of the sessions, a girl in her late teens came running toward me in sheer terror. When she finally was able to speak she said that a man in an automobile had just pulled up beside her and beckoned her to the car. She thought it was one of her fellow young people, and as she got to the side of the car he opened the door and exposed the lower part of his body to her. When she began to scream he became frightened and drove off. Later the police told us that he was an old hand at this sort of thing and that he was a married man with several small children. If he were a child we would be amused, but he was not a child and we became frightened. Something is wrong when a grown man is still unsatisfied in his childish curiosities.

The opposite of the person who exposes himself is the Peeping Tom. He is driven to find his satisfaction in looking at others who are exposed. Like his counterpart who exposes himself to people he does not know, the Peeping Tom likes to remain anonymous, too. Also, he terrifies people by staring into their bedroom windows.

People who seek sexual satisfaction in these childish ways are people whose sexual problems are symptoms of personality problems. They have not been able to feel close enough to others to share their feelings with them. In fact, they are afraid of this closeness, perhaps because they think others will not like them if they know them too well. But we all need some kind of intimate connections with others. In their emotional immaturity these people try to find some kind of "closeness" that will not hurt them. Some may "find" it in secretly watching another person disrobe. Others who are in need of attention and appreciation may stumble into the practice of exposing themselves to strangers of the opposite sex.

Perhaps you have noticed a tendency to these practices in yourself. If so, you have an idea of what may be causing it. These are problems in loneliness—particularly when it comes to having someone with whom to share your intimate feelings. These tendencies are distorted attempts to "solve" this problem. Of course, they are not even a good substitute. You want the real thing, and you can have the real thing—warm and sharing friendships with people. But it may take both work and courage to get them.

Begin right away by asking some capable counselor for

an appointment. Try explaining to him the trouble you have with your feelings. It will be hard at first because you probably are not used to talking about these things or able to recognize these feelings for what they are. As you find a confidant in him or some other capable adult, you will find it easier to share yourself with God—and finally with other people. As you become healthier in your inner person, your sexual feelings will follow suit.

Homo and Hetero

After children discover themselves as either boys or girls they enter a stage of development where boys like to be with boys, and girls with girls. During this stage, which may extend to the early teens, each may be primarily attracted to others of his own sex. Sexual curiosity and exploration may continue between boys or between girls. In a sense we can refer to this period as a homosexual period. The prefix *homo* means *of the same kind*. In contrast we use the word *heterosexual,* with the prefix *hetero* meaning *of a different kind.*

Boys who indulge in sex curiosity or sex play with each other have not reached the heterosexual stage of their development. The normal thing to expect is that, barring unforeseen interference, they will grow out of this. Unfortunately, if they are discovered, their behavior is not always interpreted in terms of their stage of development. Adults may view the situation with both alarm and repugnance, and serious reprisals against the individuals may follow. The reprisals do not do half as much harm as the stigma of being considered perverted.

Again let us shift scenes. A man is brought into the police station. He has been caught molesting boys. The police recognize him as a confirmed homosexual. Instead of being oriented as a man in his attraction for women, he not only is attracted to men but seeks to establish his sex life with men.

We say that this is unnatural because he is no longer passing through a stage in his development to a hetero-sexual orientation. He has become *fixed* on a homosexual level as an adult. We consider him a danger because in molesting young boys he injects an emotional crisis into their lives that may interfere with their normal develop-ment as healthy persons.

This same condition may exist also in women. When this is the case, the woman has become blocked in her development in identifying herself as a woman. Her sexual attractions then are for other women rather than for men. Women who are aggressive in desiring other women usually have other characteristics that show that they prefer to identify themselves with the masculine role rather than the feminine.

How can we account for such a person? The common idea is that there is something wrong with him or her physically. In some few instances this is true. But in the large majority of such people, we are dealing with a per-sonality or emotional disorder rather than with a physical abnormality. Theirs is a case of becoming "hung-up" or stymied in their development because of faulty relation-ships in their lives. There have not been the needed in-fluences in their development that encourage normal growth. Usually we think of these influences in terms of parental or other significant adult relationships. Unfortu-nately, the relationships with male and female that were available to these people in their developing years exerted a discouraging rather than encouraging influence on nor-mal growth.

Guilt and Fixation

Then there is the role that guilt plays in these fixations. It is hard enough in our culture to find a solution to guilt feelings in general, but guilt feelings about homosexual tendencies are the hardest of all to solve. When guilt has no release, it has a way of fixing us in the very thing about which we feel guilty. In our guilt over these tendencies we label ourselves perverted. Since so-called normal people seem unable to accept the homosexual, he may feel that his only way of finding acceptance is with those who are in the same state he thinks *he* is. So the mental fixation becomes more and more entrenched.

It is evident, then, that a person who feels he has homosexual tendencies is prone to despise himself. Even worse he—or she—may feel that nothing can be done to help him, and so why try? In this he is very wrong. Much can be done. But it takes courage to seek the help he needs. He will have to endure the embarrassment of telling somebody else the truth about himself. In addition to these barriers he may have a problem over his own sincerity. He may not *want* to give up his homosexual ways. Because he feels shut out from accepted society, a person with these tendencies may be in rebellion against society. He may be more concerned about not getting caught than he is about getting help.

Naturally this person lives in constant fear that people will see through him. He may even fear blackmail from those who know.

The result is that he leads a double life. The hidden side of this life he shares with no one but those who he discovers have the same tendencies as himself. What then happens to his guilt feelings? Instead of responding to them as an indication that he should change, he is more likely to try and siphon them off in religious rituals of one sort or another, or in some other type of external compensation such as compulsive bodily cleanliness or personal neatness.

It is precisely for these reasons that the homosexual person is difficult to help. He is either afraid to come for help, or he does not want it. When he finally does seek help it may only be because he has been caught. As part of his "punishment" he submits to treatment. But because he has developed such a pattern of deception in covering up, he finds it difficult to be honest not only with the professional counselor, but also with himself. All the time he is supposedly receiving help he may have little real intention of giving up his secretive indulgence. But once he is really sincere about wanting help—once he is more concerned about overcoming his problem than about not getting caught in the future—the chances are good that he will receive the help he needs. And the sooner he gets down to business with his problem, the better are his chances for working out the solution.

Not everybody who asks for help asks because he really wants help—at least not at first. The immediate reason Ray Fisher came to see me was that his school authorities referred him. In spite of his attempts to keep his homosexual activity hidden, "it had gotten out." When Ray arrived his defenses were up. He had never confided in anyone. The very thought of talking about his problems to a counselor was enough to send chills up and down his spine. But talk he did.

He talked about many things that had happened in his past. He told about his problems at home and at school and how he felt uncomfortable with groups of fellows and preferred the company of one or two "who were like I was." He told about how he was introduced to homosexual experience by a young man who was a little older than he. Ray had continued off and on in this practice, and even admitted that he himself had been aggressor on some of the occasions.

After we had come this far in our relationship something seemed to go wrong. Ray began arriving late for his appointments and insisted that he had to leave early— and while he was present he was obviously ill at ease.

It was Ray himself who finally brought things to a head. After a very unsuccessful interview in which he said hardly anything, he rose to leave. We were wondering about our next appointment. He hesitated for a moment and then slowly lifted his eyes to mine and said, "I'm wondering whether we are going to be able to accomplish much more."

"Does it seem to you that we aren't getting any place?" I asked.

"No, it's not that—well, yes, maybe. Here's the point. I'm just wondering whether I'm really putting myself into this."

"How do you mean, Ray?"

"Well—I've done so much covering up," he said. "I've cheated on God. Now I'm really cheating on you. I've led a double life for so long, I can't even tell when I'm sincere."

"I suppose it is hard even to be honest with yourself," I said.

"Frankly I don't even *know* myself," he said. "I know I get very uncomfortable in here when we talk about me."

"Can you recall anything particular that made you uncomfortable?"

"Well—the whole business does," he said. "I feel as if you were trying to trap me—to control me—and I don't want you to."

"Is it like giving up—or surrendering to me?"

"Yes. I guess I want to live my own life. But that's foolish. What am I here for if I don't want to change? I guess it's because I've never felt I *could* live my own life—in the past, that is."

"Homosexual experience itself is a form of non-conformity, isn't it?"

"Yes, I guess it is," he said thoughtfully.

"Because you have never felt you could live your own life in the past, you feel you have to fight for it now."

"And I've found ways of doing it too," he said. "You know if you keep talking, you can finesse a person out of position—if you know what I mean." Ray smiled a little as though he were trapping himself. "Maybe that's what I'm doing now—with you."

"What position do you want to avoid now?" I asked.

"You asked me what made me most uncomfortable. I know what it is. It's when we get talking about religion. I don't know why—yes, I guess I do. I've got to level with God—and with you."

"And this you don't feel you have been doing."

"No," he said, "it's easier to keep going the way I was. I'm afraid of girls. They seem to get along all right with me. I can be sarcastic about them and to them—but I think really it is because I am afraid of them."

"You mean afraid of them in terms of your role as a man."

"Yes—that's it precisely. And for me it's easier to take the path of least resistance. I've never assumed much responsibility or done anything that's taken much courage.

I guess that's why I wanted to quit coming here. I'm going to have to want to change—and that's going to take courage."

"And you are wondering whether you have it."

"Definitely," he said. "But I'm glad we've talked this over. I realize now—I dare not quit. I've got to go through with this now—or it may be never—and that I wouldn't want!"

Now Ray is ready for help.

What is the treatment for homosexuality? Again we are dealing primarily with a personality problem. Sexual immaturity—and this is what homosexuality is—is one sign of a general emotional immaturity. The avenue of help for such a person lies in exploring himself with some professional person who has a good understanding of the nature of homosexuality, such as a psychiatrist or clinical psychologist.

But there is also the religious problem of guilt that keeps him from looking into himself. He needs to talk this over with his pastor so that he may receive the forgiveness of God, and receive it to the extent that he can forgive himself. When he has in this way come to peace with himself, he is on the way to recovery. As he continues in the counseling relationship he will begin to see why he is emotionally immature—as Ray was doing—and also what has been lacking in the way he has gotten along with the people in his life.

An individual who has a problem similar to Ray's needs to be scrupulous in his determination to identify all that is going on within himself, so that the defensive habit of deception—including self-deception—will begin to break down. If he is determined to solve his problem, the benefits received from his counseling relationship will help him grow more secure in his inner life and in his life with other people. The positive relationship he develops with the counselor will strengthen him in developing wholesome relationships with others.

So treatment for homosexuality is a matter of obtaining the right kind of help and through it an understanding of the influences that have been at work in the formation of the problem. It is also a matter of determination to overcome, of strict honesty with God, self, and people, of courage to make changes, and of faith in God's power.

When a person is making progress in these objectives, something positive will happen. He is growing into a more wholesome and mature personality and his sexual tendencies will begin to re-route themselves in line with his growth. In the meantime of course he grows in his ability to control his actions in line with his own best interests as well as the interests of society.

The Ordeal of Being Approached

Let us take a look into what often happens when a young person is accosted by one of these disturbed adults.

Bob's folks took in roomers. One of these was a young graduate student who took a particular interest in Bob. Bob himself was barely fourteen at the time and somewhat slow in his development. His mother and father both worked, and since they were very busy, they were pleased that the young man was showing an interest in Bob. One day the young man invited Bob to his room to see some of his curios. While they were apparently engrossed in curios he began to talk rather intimately with Bob and made a homosexual advance. Bob was at first confused and then terrified.

He broke away from the young man and ran downstairs.

He was so upset that he was awake all night; yet he never told his parents. He was afraid to—afraid of what they should say or think—about *him*. Despite the fact that it was he who had been accosted, he felt strangely guilty about the whole thing, as though he were defiled. Along with the shock of the experience, Bob had also been stimulated sexually. When the young man realized that Bob had not told his parents, he tried to get Bob alone again. The result was that Bob lived in an emotional upheaval of fear and guilt until the student finally moved out.

Madge was already seventeen when she was accosted. She was a very friendly girl, one who "never knew a stranger." At a dance one evening she met a married man older than she and was friendly to him. About a week later he stopped and gave her a ride home from school. This happened four or five times.

Madge had a feeling he was "making passes" at her, but she did not know quite what to do about it. One day he drove her in another direction from her home and stopped in an isolated area. He began to force his attentions on her and when she resisted, he threatened her. When he finally took her home he again threatened her with physical harm if she told anybody. Although her family could tell that something was wrong, Madge was afraid to tell them what had happened, not only because of his threats, but also because she felt terrible shame over the whole incident. For months she lived in fear of seeing him again.

We have seen how God intended the sex relationship to be the vehicle for the expression of love. How then can we explain the forced attack on Madge? This is an example of human perversion. What God intended as a channel of love can become a channel of hate. When this is the case, sex is used to degrade, to subdue, to attack.

Love and hate are the exact opposites. Yet they have a similarity in passion. When sex is used as an outlet for hate, it apparently softens the hostility, but the end result reveals brutality.

What to Do?

Of course these are the unusual things that happen rather than the usual. But the fact that they can happen and that they do happen to some young people leads us to ask how we may avoid them. In attempting to answer this, there is always the danger that we become overly anxious about these things. The fact that thieves may break into your house should not cause you to stay awake all night in fear; yet it may lead you to lock your doors. So in a comparable way we are suggesting some precautionary measures.

While nobody would want you to become unfriendly, there is such a thing as being cautious in your friendliness. Jesus said, "Be wise as serpents and harmless as doves." Most people are worthy of your trust. But some are not. When people whom you do not know very well become overly friendly, showing an unusual interest in you, take it easy in responding. Be kind and considerate, yes, but in this same spirit, say no to invitations or suggestions that demand your trust before it has been given a chance to develop. You may have a natural tendency to be uncritical in these things when you are lonely and desirous of company. You may also be the kind of person who finds it difficult to say no when another wants you to say yes. These are weaknesses we need to come to grips with so that we do not allow them to destroy either the wisdom or the freedom of our judgment.

It is not only of people we need to be cautious, but

places also. If you are not sure about the company you are with, stay where there are other people around. Avoid dark and deserted streets, parks, or the countryside— places where shouting would do you no good. Avoid going to the person's room or house if no other responsible person is around. Also, when you are by yourself avoid isolated and lonely places, especially at night. Even when you are with your sweetheart, you take a risk when you frequent lonely "lovers' lanes."

But the fact that we take these precautions cannot guarantee that we will not be faced with such a situation. It can happen even when we least expect it. It may be helpful therefore to give a few suggestions concerning what to do if you should ever be accosted by a sex deviate.

First of all, try to remain as calm as you can, both inwardly and outwardly. This is a time to think, not to panic. Sometimes by keeping outwardly casual you can talk a person out of his intentions, or at least distract him enough to slip away or otherwise outwit him.

Sometimes girls find that a healthy scream will frighten the offender away, particularly when there are people within hearing distance. But this also has its dangers. When some of these individuals are threatened with being caught, they too may panic and become violent in defense. The best advice is to keep your head so that you can be alert for opportunities to distract and dissuade.

After such an experience a person is pretty well shaken up emotionally. Yet he may feel ashamed to tell anybody. This is a mistake. Go to your parents about it. If you feel you cannot do this, go to some parental substitute such as your pastor or teacher. You need to get this thing out in the open so that it does not cause you any more trouble than is necessary. When we keep these things to ourselves, they tend to become "infected" and cause greater harm. After you have talked it out, remember that your "accoster" is in need of help. He is a disturbed person, perhaps even a sick person. He needs your prayers.

Concerns About Yourself

Perhaps in all of this discussion you have been wondering whether *you* are sexually normal. This is to be expected.

As I have mentioned, we differ in our rate of development. Just as little children need to feel secure with the members of their own family before they are ready to step out into the world of strangers at school, so in our development into adolescence we need to feel secure and at ease in our relations with those of the same sex before we are ready to enter the more mature role of attractiveness to the opposite sex. During this transition we may have some peculiar sexual impulses which both confuse us and make us feel guilty. The thing to remember is that by and large these impulses are associated with passing stages in our development. As we mature we grow more settled also in our sexual nature. If you continue to be disturbed about yourself, seek out a competent adviser such as your school counselor. It may be reassuring just to talk the matter over.

This is what Arthur Thomas did. In Arthur's own words, he felt he had an "anemic personality." He had grown up under the domination of his mother, upon whom he leaned quite heavily, largely because he was afraid of his father, who was both harsh and quick-tempered. The fact that he seemed to develop more slowly than other boys bothered him. By the time he was a senior in high school he began to have fears that he was different from other boys.

"I don't seem to feel the same way—I mean, sexually—about girls as other boys do," he said.

"You notice a difference between the way they talk and the way you feel," I said.

"I don't feel that way toward girls," he said. "When I think of marriage I get scared. I seem so different. I've never really gone around with fellows much. I'm afraid I can't hold my own with them. When it comes to sports, I've just never gone in for them."

"And so you feel unable to compete."

"I'll tell you what really frightens me," he said. "The other day when I was watching one of my classmates show off his muscles—it bothered me some—I mean, I was sexually aroused."

"And you are wondering why?"

"Well—yes—I suppose its because he is the way I'd like to be—I mean, he's a real male."

Actually so was Arthur. It was just that his sheltered existence had not encouraged his natural potentialities to develop. He was afraid to be himself. In the course of time he grew stronger as a person by learning to express himself, to deal directly with his resentment toward those who dominated him, and to develop his own leadership abilities. It was only a year or so later that he felt he was pretty well straightened out.

"I felt inadequate," he said. "Emotionally I was blocked. Because of this I suppose you could say my sexual nature was misdirected. But as I developed a fuller life—you know, mixed more with others and straightened things out

with my folks—well, I found I'm just as normal as anybody else."

"It was a matter of being a man in spirit."

"That's the way I see it," he said. "I had to become strong
enough to be honest—with myself first and then with
everybody else."

8

Wholesome Dating

To get back from sexual deviations to the role that sex plays in the relationships of dating, courtship, and marriage, our subject in this chapter is the date.

We are going to talk about dating as a whole. Sex is not something that is off by itself, separated from the rest of our life. Rather it is something that is very much influenced by our attitudes and actions in the whole of life. Therefore let us take a look into the kind of dating that is helpful to a wholesome expression of affection.

Attitudes Toward People

If the character of our dating as a whole has something to do with how we handle our expressions of affection, what is really involved is our attitude toward people. You probably know some people who seem to be interested in others only for what they can get out of them. They are interested in certain things *about* a person, but they are not interested in the person as a *person*. We can describe this attitude as treating another as though he were a thing—an "it." We try to use people—exploit them, manipulate them—to serve our own self-centered purposes. In contrast to this attitude we may also treat another as though he were a "thou"—another human being with a world inside of him like our own. When we view another as a *thou* we go beyond any part of him, or thing about him, to see him as a whole.

Cartoonists have unusual insight into the foibles of human nature, and they make fun of us. They recognize this tendency of ours to think of a person in terms of his parts rather than his whole, and they draw him as though he were only a part. Taking an outstanding characteristic such as a beautiful figure, a head of hair, lots of money, a big car, big brain, or the like, they draw the person as though this characteristic were all he had. The result is a caricature. The picture is so distorted and out of proportion that it is not the person at all. It is ridiculous—and so we laugh.

The more serious side of seeing people in terms of a part is that the part we see may be the part we are most interested in *using*. The youngster in a neighborhood who has a pony is "the kid with the pony" so far as the other youngsters are concerned. Why? Because they want to ride the pony. Suppose the pony dies? How will he fare as "the kid without a pony"?

Vernon saw the problem from the other end. He felt left out and ignored by other young people. Perhaps if he had plenty of money to treat the kids, things would be different. The next day he treated the boys at the corner to banana splits. A couple of days later he paid their way into the best show in town. He discovered that if he offered to fill the tank with gasoline, they took him along in their car. Vernon was "getting in." But it all came to a sudden halt one day when Vernon was called out of class. He had been stealing the money.

Using people for what they can do for us is a characteristic of self-centered living. It causes us to govern our approach to people on the basis of how they may fit into our plans for getting what we want. This is the case whether it is a ride on a pony, sexual gratification, or a promotion in business. When the person's usefulness is over, we lose interest in him. The fact is we were never really interested in *him*. The world was full of "its" with only one "thou"—ourself.

Sexual Exploitation of Others

When people are tempted to use others for their own purposes, they have not been satisfied in their basic needs and are trying to find their satisfaction in this self-centered way. Much of the "uncontrollableness" of our sex impulses is explained in this way. As we have seen, every child has a natural curiosity regarding his own body and the bodies of others, both of his own sex and of the opposite sex. If his elders react with shock to this curiosity and prevent him from satisfying it, by the time he is a teenager his curiosity may be the main stimulus behind his indulgence in petting.

Darlene felt that this curiosity was partially responsible for her difficulties with sex—at least in the beginning.

"In my home," she said, "we never talked about things that had to do with sex. It was just hidden, that's all. Even though I had a brother I was terribly curious about boys. We always dressed in the strictest privacy. But it was more than this. I wondered what happened when a boy and girl went together—what happened inside, in the way they feel."

"And do you think it was to satisfy this curiosity that you got into your difficulties?" I asked.

"I'm sure it was that in the beginning," she said. "But it isn't that now. I was green all right, but not any more. My curiosity is satisfied so far as that goes, and I believe I have a more mature attitude toward sex as a result. But I still have my problem—but bad!"

Darlene was a girl with high ideals, but she seemed unable to follow through on them. In her dating relationships she found herself repeatedly losing control of herself emotionally so that she lost all sense of right and wrong.

"I like to be loved, I guess," she said. "If a boy shows me affection I just let myself go. I haven't gotten pregnant yet—I've just been lucky."

"Affection means a great deal to you."

"I didn't realize it until I started dating," she said. "My family is not an affectionate family. I can only remember once when my father kissed me. That was when I was confirmed at Church."

"Is there some reason why you mentioned just your father?"

"It's the same with my mother. I don't recall either of them showing any affection with each other either. I suppose I mentioned my father because we don't get along at all."

"Oh?"

"No—we go round and round," she said. "Nobody can do anything with him. There's really no use arguing with him, but he makes me so mad I can't help it."

"Really gets you upset."

"When I leave home after one of these fights I don't care *what* happens. I get that hopeless feeling of what's the use!" Darlene got that look in her countenance that says she just thought of something. "Now that I think of it," she said, "I could have said, 'when I leave for a date after one of these fights, I don't care what happens.'"

"You mean that this attitude may have something to do with your sexual problem?" I asked.

"I seem to have two selves," she said. "The one is the Darlene that has the ideals and convictions—the believer. The other—well—when I get so I don't care, I'd like to flout all of God's laws."

"The other Darlene is the rebel, then."

"In fact—and I hate to admit this—I get a certain satisfaction in seeing how far a boy will go—particularly a good boy."

"Seeking a companion in guilt?"

"Maybe—but I think also it's that I get a sense of confidence out of it—like it was an accomplishment—like I had power."

Young people who have been denied the basic need for the assurance that they are loved for themselves may try to find this assurance through the physical expression of sex with other young people. Those who are uncertain about whether they are really men or women may try to prove their masculinity or femininity by seeking sexual experience with the opposite sex. So long as our sexual nature has to bear the brunt of these unmet needs in our development, we will be tempted to look upon others as the means for satisfying these needs through sexual expression.

How different when we view another person with respect. We are interested in him then because he is a fellow man in this great community of humanity—a neighbor whom we are to love as ourself—a person for whom Christ died. Contrast this with the selfishness in the attitude that views another in terms of what we can get out of him. When we respect the person whom we are dating, we have an incentive to both honesty and moderation in our expression of affection. It probably looks as if all respect does for us is put limitations on our affection. Actually the opposite is true. Respect adds another dimension to affection. It gives it a deeper meaning.

Freedom Depends on Character

If you lived in some of the other cultures of the world you would not have much of a chance to be with your date alone. Instead you would be accompanied by a chaperon. How would you like your girl friend's aunt to accompany you on your date? Horrors no! This is too far a cry from what we are used to.

You are living in a time of unprecedented freedom for young people, with almost a total lack of supervision concerning what goes on during the date. This is due largely to the role of the automobile in dating. The good part about this is that it gives you the opportunity to be mature and to develop responsibility. The bad part is that not everybody is equal to the challenge.

The responsibility for the kind of dating that you do rests squarely on your shoulders. Because this is a challenge to your maturity, it means you will have to make some decisions. The question, of course, is what kind of decisions will you make. Perhaps you are a person who has a hard time making decisions. If you are, you have lots of company. Decisions are not easy to make for the simple reason that decisions have consequences. The decisions we make help shape our character. Likewise the character we have has something to do with the decisions that we make.

The Necessity of Making Decisions

The trouble in making decisions may be that we want to have our cake and eat it, too. When it comes to making a choice some of us want both choices. As a result we may have to deceive ourselves a little. We make a decision, but since we want the alternative also, somehow or other we see to it that we are unable to carry through on our decision. If we really want to fulfill our responsibility we have to cut through the fogginess of wishy-washy thinking and make a decision that is a genuine decision.

It may help if we realize that what we really want we have a good chance of getting. All the suggestions that I might make—dating the right kind of person, planning our dates, broadening our interests—will be of little help in themselves. But in the hands of those who really want them to work, they may be helpful in implementing our decision.

This decision will have to be made before the date, not during it. We cannot wait until the situation is upon us to decide what we are going to do because when our emotions are aroused we "think" with them rather than with our reason. But if this decision is made beforehand it continues to influence us in the midst of our emotional build-ups. What we believe governs how we act.

One day I was visiting with a young man whom I had known for several years. During the course of our conversation he told me how he and his fiancée had come to terms with the sexual problems of their courtship. Because I knew that he is a boy who would have had as difficult a time as any with this problem, and because I was impressed by the honesty and maturity of his ideas, I asked him if he would mind writing them up. He was naturally hesitant. When I told him he might be helping other young people by doing this he consented to try. He came up with the following.

Mary and I plan to be married in June. We are very much in love and feel that our relationship during courtship has prepared us for a happy married life, though we know it has not been perfect.

Courtship and love are beautiful, but they are also complicated. Following are some problems, suggestions, and possible solutions that may be helpful to you in your dating experience.

First of all, I would like to mention some of the consequences which result from necking and petting to extremes during courtship. When one goes against his conscience, there is always an undermining of self-confidence. This is an expensive price to pay. Self-confidence is a valuable thing.

Physicians tell us that excessive sexual excitation in necking and petting can cause glandular and emotional disturbances which leave the couple nervous and irritable.

The final stage of sexual excess during courtship is sexual intercourse. We have all read examples of unhappiness caused by pregnancies and births out of wedlock. This is the most expensive payment an individual can make during his youth. Even more important, sexual intercourse before marriage is a gross sin in the sight of God. It's a sin because it's selfish; it's an attempt to enjoy the privileges of marriage without taking the responsibilities. It's unfortunate, to say the least, to be forced into marriage, which should begin with God's richest blessing. God can forgive such a sin, but it is difficult to feel forgiven, and the marks of such a sin will never be forgotten.

Now that some of the dangers of courtship have been mentioned, I would like to give two principles which I feel may help you control your emotions.

1) We are HUMAN BEINGS! We are all potentially capable of going to sexual extremes. Admit that God has created within you this urge. Admit to yourself that you long for sexual completion, but don't dwell on it. Don't rely on will power alone to control your sexual urges, for this is the first step toward failure and leads to a false sense of confidence.

We are indeed human beings created with the power to procreate. But seeking sexual gratification outside of marriage is almost always a selfish desire.

2) We are INDIVIDUALS before God! Courtship is a period during which a couple try to grow closer by means of a social and spiritual relationship. There is also a danger connected with this—that the two people may tend to lose their individuality before God.

In our case, we have tried to stress this individuality. In other words, both Mary and I are individuals, answerable to God. We come to God individually when we go against our consciences, and it's pretty hard to offer an excuse to God when He has promised us strength.

Mary and I do occasionally discuss our sexual weaknesses, but we don't dwell upon them. It's my opinion that when two people discuss a common weakness, the discussion itself may become an escape. They are seeking strength in unity, but they may find only a double weakness.

Along with these two thoughts, let me offer a few practical bits of advice. First of all, pick your dates intelligently. *Consider each one a possible marriage partner.* I don't mean you should get serious on the first date, or about every date. Have fun, and lots of it. Date a variety. But keep the principle in mind.

When you feel you have found your life partner, breathe a prayer of thanksgiving to God, for this will be the most peaceful feeling of your youth. Don't hurry this relationship. Go slowly from the start, for the romance will advance fast enough normally.

I feel it's the boy's responsibility to determine the limits of affection. It's the man who *calls the cards* in the normal family today, and it should also be the masculine member who takes the yoke of responsibility in courtship. (This does not mean that the girl is released from her share of responsibility.)

The affections of a couple should be limited, but I don't think we should try to eliminate them entirely! In the first place, it's probably impossible. Secondly, I can't imagine a true romance without affectionate embraces.

But watch your imagination and daydreaming when you're apart. Don't dwell on sexual fantasies. They may turn to reality when you are again with your partner. Think twice about going steady seriously at an early age. Four years of college is a considerable length of time, and it's expensive. Be wary of long engagements, for during an engagement the emotional pitch of the romance becomes quite high.

It is my prayer that some of these suggestions may help you deal with the problems of your romance; but my ideas are certainly not the last word. Solutions may vary with individuals. Ask for suggestions from mature individuals that you know and respect.

Remember, you are responsible for your actions before God as an individual. And remember that your life is not entirely your own, but that it will some day be shared by your future husband or wife.

Planned and Varied Interests

Now that we have discussed the character of the dating relationship, what about the content of the date itself? Here we have the opportunity for a wide development of our interests. To help in making the most of this opportunity, we need to plan the activity for our dates. Planned dates are also helpful in encouraging moderation in the marks of affection. This is particularly true when two people are dating each other consistently. The unplanned date in this situation leads to the problem of "what shall we do?" When we have a vacuum like this to contend with, we are tempted to fill it by expressions of affection. An early participation in the marks of affection can lead to quite a buildup before the date is over. Therefore it is a challenge to us to plan our dates so that we do not leave ourselves open to this problem. And the steadier the relationship the bigger the challenge.

The idea in planning dates together is to develop a wide variety of interests. God has given us a great capacity for enriching our lives. As Stevenson said, "The world is so full of a number of things." It is tragic when we allow this capacity to go undeveloped and end up as narrow and shrunken as our range of interests. The time to see that this does not happen to you is when you are young.

Plan your dates so that the interests of the whole person are taken into account. The body, the mind, and the soul are all involved in composing the oneness of our person. This means that the capacities of body and mind and soul need to be reckoned with if we are to develop ourselves in the fullest sense.

Naturally some like sports better than others; some prefer serious minded literature, drama, or discussion; others prefer aesthetic pursuits such as music; and still others like group entertainments such as folk dancing, parties, and the like. We need to temper our own interests so that we also take into ourselves the interests of our companion or companions. If we give ourselves half a chance we will discover that we actually become interested in things that normally, because of our background, we would scarcely consider.

I have known young people who had little interest in sports until they were persuaded to try them by a dating companion; others who felt out of place and inadequate in discussing the serious issues of religion, politics, and society, until encouraged to try by a friend; still others who never appreciated music and the arts until introduced to their value by a sweetheart. If you will investigate the social, religious, and cultural opportunities that are offered by your church, your school, your YMCA and YWCA, and your community, you may find them a real help in your planning.

If you are the boy in the romance, do some creative thinking about the kind of activities you and your girl could participate in. If you are the girl and your boy friend simply asks for a date without mentioning the activity, ask him what activity he has in mind. If he appears in need of help and asks for your ideas, have a suggestion or two ready. But be careful not to take over in this area. It is a responsibility he should not forfeit. So your job is to stimulate, through ideas and encouragement, his own participation in the planning.

Once in a while a couple may complain that there is nothing for them to do in their community. This means they have the greater challenge for their ingenuity. What opportunities do the outdoors offer? How about Church activities? If they are inadequate, have a talk with your minister as well as other young people in the church. Keep up with what is going on by reading your newspaper—

also the newspapers of neighboring communities. Talk the problem over with each other and each assume responsibility for ideas and be responsive to the suggestions of the other. Sometimes the problem is more in our own negative attitude toward trying new things than it is in the absence of opportunities.

Perhaps a few of the girls can get together and plan a series of socials with their boy friends, alternating in each other's homes in the winter months and in local picnic and park areas in the summer. If you feel your community as a whole needs to provide more opportunities for its youth, talk it up among interested and influential adults. You may start something very worthwhile.

All the efforts you put forth are good practice for your ingenuity. This will stand you in good stead for the future. Married couples have to work at this same project so that their life together may be full and enriching. Their social and recreational problems are similar to yours. The more you learn how to deal with the problems in courtship, the more your married life will profit.

A well-rounded program of activity for our dates makes for a wholesome social experience. It also helps us to develop things in common with our friend. By developing more common interests through a well-planned dating experience, we get to know each other so much better. If we have any hopes that the person with whom we are dating is the person we may some day marry, we are laying a solid foundation on which to build this hope. On the other hand, if our efforts to develop more common interests meet with failure, we have a fairly good sign that we do not have enough in common to build a good marriage. And this, after all, is the major purpose of a courtship.

Accepting Limitations

As we have noted before, more than planning our dates is needed to insure moderation in the marks of affection. Nor can we expect a simple balancing of activities to relieve the courtship of its incompleteness. It is always hard to accept limitations, even when we can see the wisdom of them.

This was the position in which Sigrid found herself. She and Don had gone with each other for almost two years and planned to marry. Don had ambitions to become a lawyer, but because he was only in his second year of college, he explained to Sigrid that he thought it would be to the best interests of his education to wait until he entered law school before they got married. Sigrid saw the wisdom of it—logically she was convinced—but she did not like it at all. All her girl friends were getting married and she wanted to get married too. She hated the fact that Don's educational plans stood in the way.

Yet she could not bring herself to say anything, because when she tried she sounded so selfish that she gave up. Even to admit her resentment to herself made her feel like a "heel." As a result her resentment went underground where it began to irritate her in many ways.

Sigrid became increasingly resentful toward Don for little things which previously she could easily accept. They began to quarrel and she was in a pouty mood about half of the time. The conflict came to its crisis in their show of affection. When Don would attempt to limit the duration of their love-making, Sigrid became very resentful. She accused him of not caring for her. Probably she would have broken up with him had they not been able to talk the whole thing out one night, and Sigrid was able to face and express her resentment at having to postpone their marriage.

Once she was able to show how she really felt she was much more able to accept the situation. Don, on the other hand, also saw things better and offered to go Sigrid's way. He suggested they get married regardless. This time it was Sigrid who suggested the postponement. When she no longer felt coerced against her will, she began *really* to see the wisdom of waiting. From then on she was able to accept the limitations of their situation, though she never learned to like them.

The longing that sweethearts have for a more intimate union—the complete union—is natural and good, even though it can be agonizing. If we seek to alleviate the agony by increasing the intimacy of our love-making, we only make the agony worse. The demand for completion is simply that much greater, and the frustration that much more intense. When increased intimacy becomes habitual, it proves no more satisfying than the previous expression.

When we accept the limitations imposed on our relationship as the lesser of two evils, we are putting ourselves at an advantage in keeping the aggravation of this limitation to a minimum. With this understanding in mind, we find that as we attempt to deepen the range of our common interests as a couple, we are helping to keep our love-making in line with a relationship that is not yet prepared to accept the responsibilities that go with married life. There is less need for us to use the physical expression of affection to make up for other lacks in our development if we pay attention to these lacks directly. At the same time our attempts to broaden and deepen our relationship in the many areas of life create a better basis for marriage.

9

What Is Marriage?

What is marriage? I am sure you have an answer. Or do you? You could give a definition: marriage is the situation of a man and woman living together and, as a result, possibly raising a family.

But what are their feelings about marriage? What are yours?

In this book I have made an issue about marriage as a goal toward which our development as men and women is headed. Anything we look forward to as a goal exerts a pretty big pull on us now. Therefore our ideas and feelings about this goal are very important. Let us take a look at marriage, then, and see how it fits into our present thinking.

Companionship and Partnership

As we have seen in the creation story of the Bible, marriage is first of all an answer to loneliness. "Then the Lord God said, 'It is not good that the man should be alone; I will make him a helper fit for him.' " [1]

[1] Genesis 2:18

Marriage is a companionship; not just an ordinary companionship, but the most intimate companionship of all. Marriage is a partnership; not just an ordinary partnership, but the most complete partnership of all. The helper fit for man is not simply a helper in this or that venture, but a helper in living. The mates share life together. It is the most creative togetherness in the world. Husband and wife in their union together bring forth new life. By becoming partners with each other they become partners with the Creator. The mates are honored with parenthood. So you can look forward to marriage as the most wonderful of all human relationships—and the most challenging.

Marriage No Cure-all

It is the most challenging because all of these fine things that can come through marriage are not simply dumped into our laps when we take the wedding vows. The benefits of marriage come to us as they come in other experiences of life—through working at it. And there is a point where even marriage cannot take us. In spite of all the fine things one can say about marriage, we can also say *too* much. We can expect from it what it cannot give. Marriage was never meant to satisfy all the needs of the human personality; nor should we ever look forward to it as the cure for all of our problems.

This is exactly what Bill Black did. Because his great fear was that he would end up as a failure, he continually kept himself in an emotional dither. Always he was dissatisfied. He could not seem to go ahead on things; yet he would beat himself up mentally for hanging behind. He alternated between thinking he deserved nothing and thinking he deserved everything. When he was depressed he thought he was inferior to everybody and when he was elated he thought he was superior to everybody.

Although Bill knew he needed help, he felt all would be well as soon as he married Cathy. Marriage for him appeared to be the solution to everything. And so they were married. It was not too much later that Bill had problems, only now they were a "new" kind—marital problems. He felt that Cathy was not responsive to him— that she did not understand him. Half of the time he made himself miserable by doubting whether Cathy really loved him, and the other half he made himself miserable by thinking that she was not good enough for him—that he could have done better. As you can see it is the same old problem. Only now it has a new setting—a marital one.

The Marriage Dream

Bill was not wholly to blame for his unrealistic attitude toward marriage. There are many influences in our environment that encourage such ideas.

When we were little we listened to fairy tales about the prince and princess who married and lived happily ever after. In the movies we see this same thing time and again. After many troublesome experiences the hero or heroine finally finds the one for whom he was meant, and as they go to the altar the story ends—the idea being that marriage is the end of the road, the experience after which only happiness can reign. Fortunately, however, we have seen enough of real-life marriages to know that it is not so. Yet the dream persists—perhaps because we want it to persist.

It is all well and good to have a dream. We need dreams to keep us optimistic and idealistic. Marriage is the greatest and in a sense the last big change to which we look forward. It is essential that our dream of marriage be positive and inspiring. But when the dream of marriage has no place in it for the differences and conflicts which always occur when people live together, it may be more of a hindrance than a help. It can only lead to disappointment when the dream becomes the real thing.

On the other side of marriage there is no dream. Marriage is not heaven—no more than our sweetheart is God. Some ministers will frankly tell the couples who come to them to be married that if they expect to receive from their marital partner what only Jesus Christ can give, they are going to be disillusioned. We expect too much from marriage when we expect too much from our marital partner. In his dream Bill had made an idol out of marriage and out of Cathy, and, as they always do, his idols let him down.

The Desire for God

The incompleteness that lovers feel before marriage is never fully eliminated in even the best of marriages. This is because the feeling of incompleteness is made up not only of the desire for union with the loved one, but also of the desire for union with God.

As St. Augustine said, "Thou hast made us for Thyself, and the heart of man is restless until it finds its rest in thee." The psalmist in the Bible says, "As the hart panteth after the waterbrook, so panteth my soul after thee, O God." Anton Boissen says that even in sex our love seeks not just the other person but God, and when it ceases to do so it is no longer love.

Our experience of fellowship with God is always incomplete in this life. Our longing for it is a longing for our eternal destiny. This means that if we are going to keep our dream of marriage in line with reality, we will need to envision not only life with our marital partner, but life with God.

Building the Cathedral

Marriage is a developing experience. The wedding itself can be likened to a contract to build a cathedral. Of course, some building has been going on during courtship. Yet it is after the vows have been taken and the marriage consummated that the building is begun in earnest. And the building goes on all through marriage. Husband and wife are working at it all the time. The honeymoon is not the climax; it is only the beginning; and we would expect it to be as beginning things are.

Mark Twain said that nobody knows what perfect love is until he has been married twenty-five years. I have not been married twenty-five years, but I have been married long enough to know what Mark Twain meant. Year by year married people get to know each other, love each other, and live with each other, more and more deeply. The cathedral goes ever higher.

What of the romance of courtship during marriage? Does it continue? *Eros* remains if it is accompanied by its partners, *philia* and *agape*. In a good marriage *philia* and *agape* both deepen. When this happens, *eros* deepens also. The sexual side of marriage, as an expression of love in its fullness, continues to grow. It contributes to the deepening of devotion between husband and wife. It goes with the building of the cathedral.

Marriage Is for the Mature

Marriage is for grownup people. Children are not capable of it. Almost everybody agrees with this point of view. The trouble is that some people have grownup bodies but are still children in the way they feel and act. We say they are emotionally immature. They are not ready for marriage because they cannot give of themselves; they feel too poor inside to part with *anything*. In other words they have a hard time loving.

Perhaps you caught a glimpse of yourself in this description of an immature person. I hope you did because we are all afflicted with these symptoms to a greater or smaller degree. Loving is the very thing we all have a hard time doing. We confuse it with so many other things. We think it means manipulating people, controlling them, getting them in one way or other to do what we want them to do. Wives talk about wrapping their husbands around their fingers; husbands speak about talking their wives into things; parents talk about *managing* their children. When all this is said and done, we are still a long way from loving.

It helps us to recognize this immaturity. As one man said: "I read in all these articles and books that what my wife and children need most from me is love. And here is my frustration! For when they are most in need of my love, I find them most unlovable." If this realization does nothing more, it has already made him humble toward his task. It ought to make him more understanding toward others in the family when they have *their* difficulties.

Be Humble Toward Differences

It helps to have a humble attitude toward the differences that exist between us and others. Marriage, we say, is two becoming one. To which it is possible to retort, "Yes, but which one?"

Here is a problem. This business of two different people

becoming one flesh and one spirit is a big order. And it is not solved when one of them simply fades out and lets the other take over. The marriage cannot develop when one dominates the other because neither of the partners is himself able to grow. Nor can either of them like himself or the other under such an arrangement. The person who adopts a peace-at-any-price policy in his marriage is stultifying the growth of the marriage. He is really settling for something less than marriage. It is much better to have the differences out in the open, even if it means disturbing the peace. The wounds are at least open to airing and are more in line for healing and solution.

Strong wills are bound to collide when they attempt to merge. But this very collision is good experience. It can lead to a compromise that should broaden both of the parties. Ben and Wilma were bound to have some difficulty in working out their marriage. Both were individuals in their own right. Ben had a driving ambition to succeed in his business. Wilma was in some respects less mature than Ben—it was less natural for her to discipline and to sacrifice. Yet she was a broader person than Ben and had a wider interest in a variety of things.

Naturally there would be conflict. It erupted over their use of time and money. They brought it out into the open but they could not seem to settle anything—in fact they could not seem to stop the argument once it had started. There was never any discussion about divorce. They accepted this as part of the "worse." But they knew they needed a referee and that is how I got into the fray.

Before I realized what was happening, they were scrapping in front of me. You know how it is—something like what your dad and mom might do—charge and countercharge! Since I was not emotionally involved in their problems I could help each one in the midst of the heat to see more clearly into what he or she was agitated about. The result was that they were soon talking like two sane people. As time went on, each became more concerned about *showing* understanding than *demanding* it as they had before.

Each had to change somewhat—and for the better. Wilma had to become more concerned about economy, even to the extent of sticking to a budget. Also she had to become more aware of the importance Ben placed on his business as a career, so that she could show the necessary understanding that a husband needs from his wife. Ben on the other hand needed to become less concerned about his business so that it did not consume his entire time and interest. He needed to become more concerned about living a balanced life, for his own sake as well as for Wilma's.

So there was conflict. Out of it came not only resolution but also growth. In fact it is through the tensions of conflict that the way of growth operates. Ben and Wilma had a conflict in their marriage because neither of them was content to go separate ways. They *cared* to be one. They wanted their marriage to be all that they could make of it under God.

There will be times of disharmony in any marriage that has any vigor. The challenge is not to avoid these disharmonies but to face them openly. It is in this way that they may be used to strengthen the marriage. "Iron sharpeneth iron; so a man sharpeneth the countenance of his friend," [2] says the Bible. So, we may add, a husband sharpens the countenance of his wife, and the wife the countenance of her husband.

Being humble toward our differences means that we

[2] Proverbs 27:17

consider our own shortcomings as well as those of the other. Some people go at these conflicts like the little boy whom Abraham Lincoln told about. He and a friend were having a difficult time trying to ride on one hobby horse. Finally in exasperation he turned to the other little fellow and said, "You know, if one of us would get off, I could ride better."

So we seem to be saying, "One of us has to give in, and I am sure that when you do, you will see that I am right." Obviously if what is sauce for the goose is sauce also for the gander, this is a very unsatisfactory way of dealing with differences. The mature person would at least consider the possibility that he too might be wrong.

All of our experiences can be helpful for our growth if we are courageous enough to look at them squarely. We can learn a lot from them all. Growing in oneness both as individuals and as a married couple is not a steady climb upward. Rather it is a series of ups and downs. If we cannot take the downs, there will be no ups. For it is out of our struggle with the downs that we receive what we need to go up. And each *up* is a little more *up* than the last one. We begin growing into oneness already in our courtship when we deal directly with our differences. It is a lifetime process of give and take—of knocking off the rough edges. The experience of working out these conflicts together is in itself almost as valuable to our growth as the compromises or solutions at which we arrive.

Ability to Accept Another

The challenge to maturity in marriage is the challenge to accept another even at those times when he is disagreeable to us. This is the kind of love that is patterned after God's love. He loves us even when we are unlovable. When St. Paul wants to give instructions concerning marriage he uses this very analogy. "Husbands, love your wives as Christ loved the Church and gave Himself up for her." It is this sacrificial love of Christ that moves us in the Church to respect and follow him. So it is this same kind of love in the husband that moves his wife to respect him as the man of the home. "Wives, be subject to your husbands, as to the Lord. For the husband is the head of the wife as Christ is the head of the Church, His body, and is Himself its Savior. As the church is subject to Christ, so let wives also be subject in everything to their husbands." [3]

People prosper when they receive God's love, and we also prosper when we receive a love like this from a mate. Such an exchange of love creates an atmosphere that is favorable to growth. The same goes for the children that are products of the marriage. It is easy to have a preconceived notion of what our child is going to be like—particularly our first one. Before we know it our child is becoming an extension of our own ego. We want him to be a better child than we were. We want him to succeed where we did not do so well. And so we begin to control and manipulate him toward this end. We are not accepting him as he is. The little tyke has become an *it* rather than a *thou*. When we accept him as God has accepted us, we will respect his little personality, knowing that he can teach us even as we can teach him. In other words we leave room for God to be his parent also. We will allow him to be something less than perfect.

[3] Ephesians 5:22-24

Emotional Changes in Marriage

Maturity in marriage is needed to deal patiently with the common problems of life. Once you are married, life is different, of course. Yet you should not be too surprised if the problems that you have now crop up then, too. This is because they are common problems—they go with being human—they go with living.

Even as you get emotionally in a rut now with the routine of doing the same thing day in and day out, so you will have these routine blues then. Perhaps you felt that this is one thing that could not happen in marriage. Dating is exciting. How, then, could one ever get bored after he is married? The answer is that marriage is more than one big date.

The Strattons found this out after their first baby was born. The little fellow was as cute as any baby, but after a good start he began having one bout of ear or intestinal infection after another. This not only meant having a crotchety baby; it meant sitting in doctors' offices and paying doctors' bills.

After several weeks of exhausting her time and energies in caring for the baby, Mrs. Stratton became very weary of it all. At the same time Mr. Stratton was having his problems at the office. Although he knew it well enough himself, he had to listen many times to his wife's complaints that he was not making enough money. There was a chance for a promotion and with it a raise, but there were two other men waiting for that same promotion. Every day something happened to give him hope or to dash his hopes. When he returned home at evening weary and agitated, he found his wife in the same state of weariness and agitation.

To put it mildly, neither was much help to the other. Mr. Stratton knew that his wife needed to "get away," but with his small salary and their large bills, he felt he could not afford to hire a baby sitter and take his wife out. Besides, he was tired and discouraged. His wife's complaining made him feel guilty and worthless. On the other hand she saw in his lethargy one more reason for feeling sorry for herself. As much as she hated it, she was beginning to look upon their little apartment as a prison and her marriage as the cause of it all.

The Strattons survived this period of trial. Spring came, the baby grew healthier and therefore happier, and Mr. Stratton got his raise. But as they look back they both agree that it was a tough time in their life together. Some of it was caused by their own faulty attitudes. But much of it was the result of circumstances beyond their control. Marriage includes sickness as well as health, working as well as playing, seeing the partner at his worst as well as his best. These same changeable emotions that we have now—up one day, down the next—we will have then. And so will our partner. Life together is composed of the kind of living that goes on in your own home between your mother and dad or between you and others.

It is because of this very changeableness of our emotions that love must go beyond emotions. It is loyalty that makes for enduring marriage. Loyalty is unchanging for the very reason that it is based on more than feelings. It is a matter of the total personality—of conviction. Our vows of loyalty to each other sustain our love when all the natural *feelings* of love are in their ebb rather than their flow.

How do you live with yourself when you feel all tied up inside? How do you live with somebody when you are angry at him? How do two become one when there is a block between them? Here is the challenge to maturity. The mark of a mature person is that he can accept any imperfect situation without losing his desire for the perfect. The more mature people are, the more they can talk out what is bothering them. These feelings of ours are best handled out in the open. Unfortunately some people have to wait until they become violently angry before they can do this. You can help yourself even in your courtship to develop this maturity as you and your sweetheart cultivate the art of talking things out as they come up. It is a good sign for the marriage when lovers can talk out their problems together, and in this spirit of understanding work out mutually satisfying solutions.

In-Law Adjustment

Even the thorny issue of the in-laws can be handled when people are able to talk it out. I am sure you know some joke about a mother-in-law. Everybody usually knows at least one. Why do we make so much fun of her? For one thing it helps to laugh at something you are afraid of.

This in-law business can be quite a problem. It can also be a real blessing. The reason it is a thorny issue is that marriage brings about a decided change with parents. Sometimes the newlyweds have not fully understood what this means; nor maybe have the parents. "For this cause shall a man leave his father and mother" and it is hard to "leave" home. Even people who leave geographically may be tied emotionally. Until a person is mature, he is not ready to make this transfer. Even if he leaves he may subconsciously bring his old home along, expecting the new to be merely a continuation of the old. To have married, two people have supposedly been mature enough to leave the old, and therefore are able to cleave to each other.

Parents may find it just as difficult to allow their child to "leave" home. After being responsible for the child from babyhood on up, parents may not find it natural to think of their "child" as an adult simply because of a wedding. They may not fully appreciate at first the need of the young couple for privacy and the feeling of independence. So also the young couple may not recognize how sensitive to rejection parents can be. It may take time and patience to work out the adjustment. But the results are worth the effort. Both parents and their married children have a lot to give each other.

Trust in God

Being able to deal patiently with these common problems of life comes through a growing trust in God. Much of our trouble would work itself out if we would keep from muddying the waters. It takes faith to do this. Without it we fret, and as the Bible says, fretting "tends only to evil." Trusting in God is a steadying influence in all of our human relationships, and especially in marriage. It helps us to develop the habit of happiness which does wonders for the atmosphere of any home. The more we can develop this habit in courtship, the better not only for our marriage but for our children yet to be born. Elton Trueblood says:

> The parent makes the mistake, frequently, of concentrating on the child, when he would help the child more if he would concentrate upon himself. The parent must guard, accordingly, against the danger of too much self-sacrifice. If the sacrifice is obvious it defeats its purpose. Much as we help those whom we love by performing serv-

ices for them, we help them more by being composed and happy persons. More good is done in personal relations by the habit of happiness than by obvious deeds of kindness.[4]

In the midst of the ups and downs of the common life, faith in God helps us to keep our balance. It draws our eyes from focusing only on our problems to focus also on Him. In this way He helps us to enjoy the good life that He has given us, imperfect though it may be.

[4] Trueblood, Elton and Pauline, *The Recovery of Family Life*. New York: Harper and Bros., 1952.

10

What Are You Looking For?

I imagine that as you were reading the previous chapter you began to think ahead—wondering what your own marriage might be like. Would you like to know? Of course you would. But who can know the future?

Strange as it may seem, when it comes to your marriage, you can know quite a bit about the future. Of course you may need a little help: so if you are ready let's take a look.

Looking Ahead by Looking at the Present

We are going to look ahead, but not in the way you probably expect. We look ahead by looking at the present. If you want to find out something about your future home, take a look at your present home. The family in which you now live will have its influence in the family that you someday may help create. But it is not an unchangeable influence.

We tend to go to extremes when we talk about home influences. In either extreme we are wrong. On the one hand, a girl may say: "I like George a lot. I would like to marry him. But he comes from a poor family background. Our marriage would not have a chance." Would it not be terrible if this were true? None of us would ever be able to rise above his environment. To believe this we would have to disbelieve in God.

On the other hand a boy may say: "I know Sarah comes from a very unhappy family. But what has this got to do with Sarah? I am marrying Sarah, not her family!" Ah yes—would that it were true! But unfortunately when he marries Sarah, he is also to some degree marrying her family, whether he wants to or not. For her family is in Sarah—for good or ill.

You may copy the good points of your parents as well as the bad. You may absorb the healthy attitudes of your home as well as the unhealthy. The attitudes toward marriage and family that are present in your home, for example, will have some effect on *your* attitudes toward marriage and family. Your present family relationships with your father, your mother, your sisters, your brothers, will have an effect on your relationships within your future family.

If you are a girl you have been schooled by the example of wife and motherhood that you have seen in your own mother. It would not be unnatural, then, in your future family, if you exhibited some of the same traits toward your husband that your mother exhibited toward your father. Nor would it be unnatural if as a mother you found yourself copying the ways of your own mother toward your children. This has been the pattern that you have lived with for the first eighteen or so of your vital years. You should naturally expect some of it to rub off on you.

The same is true if you are a boy. The ways of your dad with your mother and with the children are going to be an influence in your habit patterns toward your future wife and children. When this is a good influence there is no problem. But when it is not, troubles arise.

Here we go speaking in extremes again. Actually no parental pattern is all good or all bad. Even the best parent is an imperfect person and therefore an imperfect mate and parent. Not to be able to recognize imperfection in your parents is as unrealistic as not being able to see any good in them.

The Irony of It All

Probably the most ironic part of this whole business is that we should do the same things we resented in our parents. It is ironic because of all things these are the last we would think possible for us. Perhaps this is why it can happen so easily. When Mrs. Johnson's mother died, she had a hard time even attending the funeral. She hated her mother because she had deserted the family for another man. Mrs. Johnson had two children herself. Today these two children feel toward Mrs. Johnson as she did toward her own mother. For Mrs. Johnson became as dissatisfied as did her mother and broke up her home in the same way.

Then there was Mr. Rollins. He was disturbed over his role as a father. "I had always thought that I would be a good parent," he said. "This is what I can't understand."

"Where do you feel you are failing?" I asked.

"The way I treat our little girl," he said. "I can't understand it. Without warning I get real angry toward her and just have to punish her. And when I spank her I hit her so hard! It disturbs me that I can be so cruel and unsympathetic with her—when I honestly believe I love her. It just seems I cannot accept her unless she is just so."

"You feel you demand too much of her?"

"Yes—but it is more than that. I think I take other irritations out on the little child—and it makes me feel terrible when I do."

"What might these other irritations be?"

"Usually when I'm not getting along with my wife," he said. "I'm a very independent person. I've always been proud of the fact. But I see where aloofness doesn't work out in marriage."

"You say you were proud of it?"

"Yes," he said. "I suppose it all goes back to the way I was raised. My mother was a very domineering woman. I just didn't get along with her. I left home early just to get on my own and be away from her."

"You felt that this was the only way to be independent," I said.

"I never could work anything out with her. She would never listen. My wife won't either. It's bad enough to be getting criticized all the time—but if you're not given a chance to defend yourself, that's just not fair."

"I imagine you feel licked."

"That's about it," he said. "But it doesn't end there. I get all worked up inside. I'd just like to tear things apart, including myself."

"Is this when you may turn on your little girl?" I asked.

"Right. And I've noticed that a lot of it has to do with how I get started in the morning. If I get started on the wrong foot I'm no good for the whole day. There seems to be a certain way that things have to be—and if they're not, I get in a terrible frame of mind. I'm done from then on. It seems I even try to make things worse—or at least see to it that they won't get any better."

"And what might start you off wrong?"

"Oh, again—having an argument with my wife would be one thing," he said. "Or fooling around so that I don't get a good start at my job would be another. Something that makes me feel that I've failed again."

"You are very sensitive to feeling guilty about yourself," I said.

"Oh, yes. Again I suppose it goes back to the way I was raised. As I said, my mother was very critical."

"And you wanted to please her?"

"Yes, I guess I did," he said. "But I never could. I resented her very much and rebelled all I could. And I wanted to get away. But—I wanted something more than that, I know. Once—just once—she said she was proud of me. That was when I won the top prize selling newspapers. I cried when she said it." Mr. Rollins had a hard time to keep from crying again.

"In spite of your desire to be independent you are very dependent on her approval," I said.

"I know. I never felt she cared for me. I could never live up to what she seemed to want."

"And when you said your wife wouldn't listen, did you mean that she's critical of you too?"

"Maybe I'm just oversensitive to criticism," he said. "But when she starts needling me, I feel the same way I did toward my mother. I get all worked up inside and practically hate her. Funny—I even want to leave."

"It's very similar to the past, isn't it?"

"That's what gets me," he said. "There isn't any progress. I'd like to think I'm something I'm not, I guess."

"And when you fail to fulfill the ideal you have of yourself, you get very guilty and then very angry."

Mr. Rollins nodded but said nothing. His mind was obviously elsewhere. "I see it now," he said. "I'm doing the same thing to my daughter that my mother did to me."

So it is that unsolved problems in our present home may create similar problems in our new home. As we have seen, marital problems are by and large problems that existed in one or both partners before the marriage, and in the familiar family patterns associated with marriage, they emerge as marital problems. As we have also seen, this is true even with sexual problems in marriage. So it is obvious that we need to come to grips with these personal problems and family relationships before marriage so that we are at least at work on them before we enter into the creation of a new family.

Personal Problems Affect Our Choice

In fact, these unsolved problems within us may even affect our choice of a partner. This brings up the question, "What are we looking for?" The trouble—if there is any trouble—often begins right here. What we are determines what we are looking for, and what we are looking for often determines what we find. If there are strong immaturities in our personality, these will exert an immature influence in determining what we are looking for.

A young man may be still emotionally tied to his mother. To "leave" her becomes a psychological impossibility. So without really knowing it he is looking for a second mother instead of a wife. Likewise a girl may be looking for a father instead of a husband. Girls also may be tied to their mothers and boys to their fathers, so that they lack the necessary confidence to assume an adult role in marriage and parenthood. And there are those who would like to be parents rather than mates.

Some people have never matured to the point where they can think for themselves—where they can make their own decisions. They are looking for someone who will tell them what to do. There are also those who do not feel secure unless they are "running the show." They are looking for someone whom they can dominate—whom they can tell what to do. The sad fact is that these two immature opposites often find each other. When this happens they each contribute to the other's immaturity so that neither can grow.

Others feel helpless as they face life without the supports they had in childhood. They are looking for someone who will take care of them. On the other hand there are people who have a strong desire to take care of someone. Otherwise they feel useless. Theirs is the need to be needed. Again these two opposites usually attract each other.

There are young people who feel rather worthless alone. They need someone who will elevate their status. They are looking for a person who will be a "catch." As he walks down the avenue with that beautiful gal—boy, won't he be the envy of them all! These people are looking for someone whom they can possess in order to boost their ego. This feeling of inferiority can work the other way also. Because a person sees himself as such an inferior being, he may feel out of the running for most of the "catches." He recoils from competition and begins to look for someone with whom such a one as he might even rate. In other words he is looking for someone even more inferior because he does not feel he deserves any better—

and because he wants to feel superior at least to somebody. Also it is more comfortable for him to marry someone who would not aggravate his already consuming sense
of inferiority.

Marcella was overrated by her family. Because she was
able to excel in a few areas, they thought she was something extraordinary. Actually she was quite ordinary. And
when she did not experience the same acclaim from the
outside world as she did within her family circle, she was
quite shaken by it. Whenever she returned home, however, she was elevated again to the top. Yet it was a false
glory and Marcella half realized it. But it seemed as if she
did not dare to let it go. She needed it to make up for the
strong sense of inferiority she experienced outside her
home. Outside her home she needed reassurance and
needed it badly.

To what sort of person might Marcella be attracted?
Somebody who would fail to give her this reassurance? Or
somebody who would think of her as a superior person?
She found the latter in Malcolm.

Malcolm was no threat to Marcella's ego. He did not
even try to compete with her, either in achievements or
for attention. He simply assumed that she was brilliant
and that he was not. Marcella liked this dominant role and
made the most of it. When as a couple they conversed
with others, she readily referred to her achievements and
abilities. It pleased her that Malcolm offered no objection
when she made the decisions that concerned them mutually. It seemed that they both assumed that she knew best.

Malcolm was a submissive person. He had no doubts
about his inferiority. He assumed it as unquestioningly as
he assumed Marcella's superiority. But even Malcolm on

occasion could become irritated at the high-handed way in which Marcella did things. Each time, however, he quickly stifled his resentment by justifying Marcella in some way to his own satisfaction. He had rarely been able to express any feelings of resentment.

If Marcella and Malcolm should marry, he would probably continue as an accomplice in her inability to face herself, and she would continue to be an influence in keeping him undeveloped. But no one can be sure in his predictions of human behavior. God is ever at work. Crises develop. Out of these, changes may come. It could be that in the rough and tumble of day by day living, Malcolm may find it harder and harder to justify Marcella's ways. Then he will see her in a more objective light. When this happens he may leave her with few illusions about herself. We can only hope that if this should happen, Marcella will be able to take it, and accept herself for what she is in reality. If she can, Malcolm may have created some room for himself in which to grow.

Then there are those individuals who never have received genuine love. As a result they are full of inner emptiness and worries over what is wrong with them. They are looking for someone to love them and thereby to solve all their problems. When our need is so very great it is difficult for us to be discriminating in our choice. We are liable to fall hard for the first person who happens to give us what appears to be love. Unfortunately when a person has had a relatively loveless life, he is not conditioned to receive love. He may find that he has a hard time believing that he can be loved, and it is just as hard for him to see that even if he could be loved, his problems might yet remain.

Immaturity Creates Problems

Each of these immaturities in our personalities creates a corresponding distortion in what we are looking for. This in turn can cause problems later on.

Let us take, for example, the last situation we described —the person who wants someone to love him as an answer to all his problems. Lois was such a person. Because it seemed that no one had really loved her, she felt she was basically a most unlovable person. Yet she longed for love. When Ted came along and wanted to love her, Lois began to "walk on air." Heaven had finally descended to earth. But after the newness had worn off, the old doubts which were really there all the time began to raise their ugly heads. Could anybody *really* love *her*—especially if they got to know her as she knew herself.

One day Ted was late for a date. Lois tightened inside. Was this the beginning of the end, she thought? Could it really last? Was he beginning to lose interest in her? When Ted finally arrived he sensed the tension in the air. "What's wrong?" he asked. "Nothing!" she said, clenching her teeth.

It took about an hour for the cold war to be lifted. A week later they went to a party. Ted struck up a conversation with some girls seated next to him, but on the side opposite from Lois. Again the doubts came. "He can't love me! He's more interested in those girls than he is in me!" When Ted finally turned back to Lois he knew again that something was wrong.

"What is it?" he asked.

"As if you didn't know!" she retorted, her eyes blazing.

"Well I don't—tell me," he said.

"Oh, just skip it!" she said.

"What's wrong with you?" he asked in despair.

"I said, nothing! And if you are going to keep this up, please take me home!"

This sort of thing went on and on until finally one day Ted felt it was useless to go on. "Lois," he said, "obviously I don't please you. And frankly I don't know how. Maybe it would be better if we broke off for awhile." Lois was bitter. "I knew it," she said to herself. "I knew it couldn't last. It never does. Not for me!" Doubting that she could be loved, she had proceeded to prove she was right. Here is the basis for much of our jealousy. Jealousy is a sign that our need for love is so great that it threatens to be *unsatisfiable*.

By destroying what she wanted most, Lois was her own worst enemy. Yet it is rare that any breakup is the fault of just one of the parties. Why was Ted so unable to understand Lois? By his insensitivity to her needs—probably due to his preoccupation with himself—he offended her again and again without knowing it.

How can we overcome our immaturities? Progress begins when we realize what our immaturities are. But let us keep in mind that immaturity is not something some people have and others do not. Rather it is something we are all inflicted with to a greater or lesser degree. Progress therefore does not mean elimination of immaturity but progress from more to less. As we learn to recognize our immature tendencies we can train ourselves to develop an automatic resistance to them. In a sense we declare war on them.

In any war we must sooner or later take to the offensive. This means that in battling our immaturities we consciously go to the opposite extreme. For example, if a boy is tied to his mother so that he is unable to make any decisions that are not first her decisions, he'd better begin right now to think on his own, even if it means the "roof will fall in." This is what Paul had to do. His mother and father had grown apart from each other shortly after he was born. In her emptiness his mother turned to Paul for the emotional support she lacked in her marriage.

Paul had the usual share of childhood illnesses with the result that his mother became unduly anxious about his health. As a protective measure she would not permit him to do any heavy or dirty work because "he was not strong enough." With this protective attitude went also domination. She told him when to practice his instrument, what clothes to wear, when to come home from school, and with whom to associate. In adolescence when he tended to pull away from her, she became even more restrictive in the things he was and was not allowed to do. She was not aware of her selfish desire to keep her boy to herself; she honestly believed she did these things because she loved him—and she told Paul so many times.

Even though Paul chafed under his mother's protective control, he realized that life seemed too big to brave alone so long as his mother was willing to live it for him. This frightened him. He knew he had to act. He told his mother in as kind a way as he could that he had to begin living his own life.

Naturally she was hurt. She felt he was rejecting her. When she began to cry, Paul almost "threw in the sponge." But he realized that if he did, he would be right back where he started from. So instead he put his arm around his mother and told her how much he loved and appreciated her.

From then on whenever he could make his own decisions or take care of his own needs, he did—even though it was slow and hard. He tried to avoid deliberately defying his mother because he understood how she felt, and he was very careful to give her much love and affection. As time went on, she became more and more accustomed to the idea that he was growing up, and the tension began to ease. By the time Paul is ready for marriage his mother will probably be able to give him up.

When we take active steps to overcome our immaturities we are cooperating with the will of God. In Christian teaching God's Spirit is called "The Sanctifier." Sanctification is the Biblical word for growth in character. As we act in overcoming our fears and over-dependencies, we are partners with God in developing our potentialities as a person. The whole idea of the Christian life is growth. There is a goal too. It is "the measure of the stature of the fullness of Christ." [1] It is to this ideal in maturity that we are "to grow up in every way." So you can see how natural it is that we can pray to God for help in overcoming our immaturities and be confident that He will give it just as fast as we are able to receive it. The quality of wisdom, for example, which is a mark of maturity in judgment, is mentioned over and over again in both the Old and New Testaments as something special that God will give to those who ask. "If any of you lacks wisdom, let him ask God who gives to all men generously and without reproaching, and it will be given him. But let him ask in faith." [2] Asking in faith simply means that you both pray and act in a confident way and really believe that you too can become mature.

[1] Ephesians 4:13
[2] James 1:5

Wisdom from an Old Story

What are we looking for? There is a story from the Old Testament that has something to say to us in this question. It is the story of how Isaac and Rebecca found each other.

According to the custom in his culture, Abraham, Isaac's father, assumed the responsibility for finding his only son a wife. Before we become too critical of this procedure we should add that Isaac by this time was forty years old and had done precious little about the problem himself. So Abraham called his trusted servant and told him to go back to the people from which they had come and pick a wife for his son. He did not want Isaac to marry one of the daughters of the Canaanites, in whose land they lived, because of the great difference in their culture and religion.

How was the servant going to make the selection? This is what *he* wondered. He prayed for guidance.

When he arrived at the well just outside Abraham's home village, he decided that he would ask the maidens who came for water to give him a drink. The one who offered also to draw water for his camels would be a likely candidate. No sooner had he come to this decision than Rebecca arrived at the well. When the tired traveler asked for a drink she replied, "Drink, my lord." When she had finished giving him a drink, she said, "I will draw for your camels also until they have done drinking." The Bible adds almost as an aside that she was very fair to look upon.

When she had finished her task the servant gave her a present and asked her who she was. Upon hearing that she was from Abraham's kin, he thanked God and told her who he was. He asked if he could take rest in her home. She gladly took him to her home and introduced him to her family.

Then the servant "popped the question." Her family interpreted the servant's mission as from God. They were willing, and so was Rebecca. When she was ready to leave, they departed for Canaan. While they were still a long way off, Isaac saw them coming in the distance. He was meditating in the field at the time, probably praying for the Lord's guidance in this big undertaking. As he ran to meet them, Rebecca got down from her camel, took her veil and covered herself according to the custom. Isaac tenderly took her to his tent, and the Bible says that she became his wife and he loved her.[3]

Let us look at the test which the servant used to determine what he was looking for. First he wanted someone from a similar cultural background and religion. Second, his test at the well showed he was looking for someone who was naturally kind and considerate, even with strangers—one who would go beyond the customary courtesies. Third, he wanted to meet her family. He wanted to see her in her home. There are people who are nice to strangers but who are mean and cantankerous in the family circle. And fourth, he wanted her to be willing. It would seem that we could begin right here. What Abraham's servant looked for—look for and *be*.

When Judy Anderson tried to analyze what it was that attracted her to Paul, she had a hard time doing it. For one thing Paul is very handsome. This undoubtedly had something to do with it. Another thing, he has "personality." Girls were quite "taken" with him, and fellows too. Then what was causing Judy to have her doubts about their courtship? It was the way Paul and his family

[3] Genesis 24

got along. At first she sympathized with Paul when he complained about his family. But later after she had visited in his home several times she became disturbingly aware that Paul could be rather abusive in the way he talked to his family. After they had announced their engagement, Paul's sister offered Judy the customary best wishes and then said, "You are marrying a boy who is very hard to live with. Frankly, we are all glad he will soon be leaving. I thought it only fair to tell you this."

Judy herself was an easy-going girl on the surface, but inwardly she was very sensitive. It seemed the longer they went together, the more she herself was beginning to feel the rough treatment Paul gave his family. He had a way of keeping her in a continual state of upheaval. She had gone to her physician for her nerves and ended up talking about Paul.

Judy is wise in re-examining her relationship to Paul. In spite of his good public relations he had a great deal of meanness in him. He used his family as a scapegoat for the release of this meanness. He had learned when he was younger that he could bully his family in one way or another, and because he could get away with it, it had now become a behavior pattern—a habit. As his sister told Judy, he could create more upheaval in the family in five minutes than most people could generate in a day. Would Paul sooner or later treat her as he was treating his family? Would he transfer his scapegoating pattern from his present family to his new one?

These are the questions that are troubling Judy. Through her physician's suggestion she plans to have a heart-to-heart talk with Paul concerning these things. She wants Paul to face the facts. Otherwise she would rather end their relationship before they get married.

Religious Unity

Abraham wanted Isaac to have a wife of similar background to his own—one who would share his cultural and religious heritage because the family had a spiritual destiny to fulfill. God had promised to bless all nations through the generations of Abraham.

This promise has been fulfilled in our possession of the Old Testament, the coming of Christ as our Saviour, in our possession of the New Testament and in the existence of our Church. In a sense we all live under the possibility that God will bless the future generations through our progeny. So we can with good reason follow Abraham's concern that the mate we are looking for—the one with whom we would share parenthood—will share our faith in God.

When we think of religious unity we usually think of church unity. And this is important. Yet church membership in itself may mean very little so far as faith in God is concerned.

I had this brought home to me very strongly early in my ministry. A young lady asked me to perform her marriage ceremony. She was from a religious home, but her boy friend had had no religious background. Since she had heard often enough that you cannot wait until after you are married to reform your partner, she insisted that he become a member of the church before the marriage. The young man was willing.

But in the midst of his instruction for church membership he half admitted to me that his interest was more in the girl than in the church. I encouraged him to tell her this, and he did. Yet at her insistence he continued in the class and became a church member.

Shortly thereafter they were married. But they did not stay married. Before many months had passed I was trying vainly to recall this young man to his marital vows. When I reminded him of the meaning of his church membership, he said, "You know why I joined the church. So naturally it doesn't mean anything to me now."

When there is a common faith in God between the mates there is also a common attitude toward what is important and what is not. It is naturally important that people who are going to be partners in living even unto parenthood need to have not only a common sense of values, but a wholesome sense of values. There is nothing I know of that will contribute more toward this end than a personal faith in God. Each of the partners needs the encouragement of the other's faith for the continued cultivation of his own.

Once when I was visiting in a strange city I received a telephone call from a woman whose marriage I had performed several years before. After telling me of some of the tribulations that had come to her and her husband in their family life, she ended by saying: "I feel I should tell you. I haven't been going to church. My husband never had any religion in his home. I thought I could change him. But it was rougher than I thought. It was pretty hard going it alone. You know, it's surprising how it can get away from you. You just don't think the same any more. But one of these days it's going to be different."

As I hung up the receiver I wondered—would it?

Church Unity

Although church membership cannot substitute for personal faith, it is in the church that personal faith is nurtured and exercised. The church in your community is the local gathering together of the people of God. Here the marital partners join hands with the larger fellowship to worship the King and to work for the coming of His Kingdom.

The family is not a self-sufficient unit. Only in the sense that the family recognizes and experiences membership in the larger family—the family of God—can the smaller family continue in a creative and intimate relationship. It is the nature of love that it cannot be discriminating. It cannot be given to those in our own little family and withheld from others. Worshiping together with the family of God helps us to give this love, for it brings us into fellowship with the source of love. Working together with the family of God unites our own family because it unites us to a cause that is greater than our family. Families, like people, have to live for something more than themselves or they deteriorate.

In view of all that the church can do for marriage and the family—and that the family can do for the church— you can see why it is important for husband and wife to worship and work together in the same church. It is regrettable in this instance that the church of Christ is divided into denominations. For if this division extends also into the marital union, it cuts into the partnership in the very area where it is most important that they be partners, namely, in the worship and work of God and His Kingdom. And if such a division hinders marital unity, how much more will it hinder family unity when the children come along. But when mother and father and children are united in the one congregation, their own family ties are greatly strengthened.

11

Begin Where You Are

Was it disturbing to you to look ahead toward your future family relationships by looking at your present family relationships? Does it frighten you to think that your present family may pattern your future family? There may be some natural causes for your fears. For one thing, in looking ahead you would like to have the perfect marriage and family. And in looking at your present family you see it is far from perfect. It is the contrast between these two that frightens. So let us face the facts about our present and see if we can begin where we are to do something about our future.

In the first place, I think you realize that despite your fondest hopes yours will not be the perfect marriage or family. The reason for this is the same reason that your present family may not live up to your ideals. There is no such thing as an ideal family because there is no such thing as an ideal person. Family problems are bound to occur, for no other reason than that the people in the family are all imperfect, all have their faults, are all sinners.

Future Problems in Sex

Perhaps you have heard it said on occasion that such and such a couple were sexually incompatible. What is usually meant by this is that the couple are at opposite poles so far as sexual desire is concerned. In most instances the couple were not aware before they were married that they would experience this problem. It usually takes the routine of married life to bring it to the surface. The roots of the difficulty, however, extend before the marriage, and some of the symptoms were in evidence during courtship if we could have detected them.

We would naturally expect individuals to differ in their sexual desire simply because we are all individuals. Even the individual himself experiences fluctuations in his sexual desires. The issue becomes a problem in marriage when the differences are in the extreme and where there is little understanding of what is involved. Sometimes it is the wife who is more amorous than her husband. When the contrast is extreme her excessive desires may cause him physical and nervous exhaustion. More often in these conflicts it is the woman who has the least desire. She may be accused of being "frigid." The husband at the other extreme is accused of being "oversexed." Both of these accusations are usually superficial.

Let us take an example of a potential husband and wife who might conceivably have this problem. Elizabeth and Mack have been dating steadily for six months. Elizabeth's parents were divorced when she was fifteen. The conflict had been long and severe and Elizabeth was decidedly on her mother's side. Her mother is a strong-willed and domineering woman, and has been the major influence in Elizabeth's life. Her father was somewhat uncouth and had slovenly habits, particularly around the home. Having become bitter over her marriage, Elizabeth's mother was down on men in general. So far as she was concerned, men were animals when it came to the physical appetites. Under this influence Elizabeth saw sex as vulgar—something women had to put up with to keep the animal in the man satisfied.

Even though she had been given a bad impression of men and sex, Elizabeth had received scarcely any instruction concerning her own sexual development. Her first experience with the menstrual period was a shock to her. Frightened nearly to death, she went to her mother. In vague terms and with a painful expression her mother told her that this was something that women had to put up with because they were women. It is perhaps not without significance that Elizabeth's menstrual periods have always been upsetting and severe.

Because of the conflicts that wracked her home life Elizabeth was hurt inside. She found it difficult to give of herself because she was afraid that her overtures would be spurned. She became overconcerned about one bodily ailment after another which helped to excuse her from the demands of living that she felt unable to cope with.

What can Elizabeth do to help herself now? If you are a girl with some of the problems Elizabeth has, what can you do? You can begin by making every effort to get yourself straightened out on sex. Elizabeth's mother's impressions of men and of sex are biased and therefore distorted. The fact that sex can be abused does not change its essential goodness. You are made for sexual experience and enjoyment as well as the man. Your own sexual feelings are not to be rejected, for the feelings themselves are good. But they need directing. And you are in a much better position to direct them into wholesome channels if you accept their basic goodness than you are if you consider the feelings themselves to be bad.

It is one thing to get our thinking straight on these things; it may be another to get our emotions to follow. You can accept something with your intellect but still be repulsed by it so far as your feelings are concerned. It may help to get your thinking into your emotions if you condition yourself to think of sex as God's idea. When you have sexual feelings, God does not leave you. When mates who love each other experience their love sexually, God's approval and His presence are in the midst of them.

So far as your personality is concerned, your challenge is to let go of yourself. Open up rather than hold back. There is really nothing to fear—at least nothing as fearful as what holding back may do to you. Here again you may find help through a religious point of view. God desires your self-fulfillment. He wants you to let yourself out. When you would normally hold yourself in, ask God for His help. When it is clear what you can and should be doing to give expression to yourself, follow this prompting of His spirit in obedience to Him.

Now let us go to Mack. Despite his outward bravado he is inwardly plagued with feelings of inferiority. He had an older brother who was outstanding both as an athlete and as a student, and Mack felt defeated so far as ever being as much of a person as his brother. He repeatedly used masturbation as an outlet for his frustrations in competing with others. Also he is already using his romance with Elizabeth as a source of reassurance that he is of value. Because of his insecurity he is very sensitive to anything that looks like rejection. Elizabeth has noticed more than once that he can be jealous for little reason. When Elizabeth disappoints him in her response to his attentions he flares up in anger. He does not mean to hurt her, and his temper quickly subsides; but the scene shows that his own needs may make it hard for him to be considerate of hers.

What can Mack do now to help himself for the future? What can you do if you see some of yourself in Mack? Your potential sex problem is really a problem regarding your own self-worth. Therefore whatever you can do to attack the problem directly will lessen your need to find compensation elsewhere. Granted that dealing directly with inferiority feelings is a long and difficult process, it is really the shorter distance because it is straight to the point. Your need is to believe in yourself so that you can release yourself to do your best.

It may help you in accomplishing your goal to realize that you are a child of God. Your value does not depend on how you compare with your brother or with any other fellow; it depends on God's evaluation of you. And this is settled. God's whole operation of the world is based on the reality that He loves you—and Mack—in spite of your shortcomings, and wants to make of your life something really worthwhile.

But all of this is irrelevant unless it is made practical in terms of our human relationships. For both Elizabeth and Mack the real challenge lies in their day by day contacts with the vital persons in their lives. And so we turn to some of the most vital—our parents.

Parental Problems

Problems with your parents are not only understandable, they are also to be expected. In addition to the fact that both you and your parents are imperfect, there is that knotty little problem of parental discipline. Even though you may admit that parental discipline is necessary, I doubt that you always agree with your parents in their discipline, and I doubt that you like it even if you have to admit it is right. This natural dilemma is complicated by two other facts about discipline. Granted that parents are normal human beings, not all of their discipline may have the right motivations. Once I asked the superintendent of a children's home whether his institution allowed the house parents to spank the children.

"Oh yes," he replied.

"Do you think it helps?" I asked.

"Well," he said as he pondered a bit, "I know this much —it sure helps the house parents."

Perhaps at times you have felt that some of your parents' discipline was more of a release for them than a help to you. You may be right. But if it has helped your parents, it has at least helped somebody!

The other fact that complicates our feelings over discipline is our normal desire for our parents to think well of us. In moments of discipline we may feel that price is too high to pay to achieve this desire—that we are seemingly unable to please them. And so we are pushed away from the very direction that we feel pulled toward. The result of this is that twisted-up feeling inside that we call frustration.

Every boy needs his father. But not every boy feels he *has* him. Cliff was one of these. He was a seventeen-year-old with his black hair combed straight back.

"I wish I could get close to my dad," he said. "But I just can't."

"What do you think is in the way, Cliff?" I asked.

"Well, for one thing, Dad has a terrific temper. I guess

I'm half afraid of him—especially when he's been drinking. I think Mom is too."

"Afraid of him?"

"Yes—when he loses his temper, that is."

"Neither of you answers him back, I take it."

"No sir! Not me at least," Cliff replied. "Mom will sometimes, but not always. It seems this is the only kind of emotion Dad shows—anger! He's not affectionate or anything like that. He wouldn't give a compliment to save his soul—at least not to anyone in the family."

"So you never know whether you're pleasing him or not," I said.

"Well . . . I think I *know* all right. He usually criticizes what I do. I can't seem to do anything right so far as he's concerned."

"Makes you feel you're rather low in his opinion, I suppose."

"Yeah," Cliff mused. "But, y'know, it's a funny thing— my aunts and uncles tell me Dad's proud of me, that he even brags about me!"

"But he wouldn't let you know it."

"He sure wouldn't!"

"How do you feel, Cliff," I asked, "when he begins to criticize you?"

"I just feel like quitting whatever I'm doing. I don't have any desire to go on. I lose all confidence in myself right there and then."

"And how do you feel toward him at these times?"

"Well, that's hard to say. I feel he doesn't care about me, I guess. I suppose I feel angry toward him."

"But you don't show it."

"No . . . not most of the time," replied Cliff. "Once in a while I do. But then it seems to make matters worse.

Usually I keep it to myself. Sometimes I complain to Mom."

"And she's understanding?"

"Oh sure, Mom's different . . . she and I are pretty close." Cliff smiled slightly, then grew serious again. "That's another thing—I think Dad resents this. He thinks Mom and I are together against him."

"That doesn't help, does it?"

"It sure doesn't." Cliff looked deeply serious. "That's the trouble," he said quietly. "A guy should be close to his dad too, not just to his mother."

Cliff's right. Every boy needs a relationship with his dad to develop into manhood. But how is he going to get it?

It's just possible that Cliff's dad wonders at times what Cliff thinks of *him*, and he may even be troubled by it. But he would never let anyone know, least of all Cliff. It simply isn't his way of doing things.

For another thing, Cliff's dad is having a hard time, too. People who are at peace with themselves don't go around belittling others. Instead of saying, "What's wrong with me?" when his father belittles him, Cliff needs also to ask, "What's eating Dad?" In this way he's not only getting a more realistic understanding of the situation, but he'll overcome his fear of his father.

Parents Feel Guilty Too

My experience in counseling with both young people and parents in these problems is that both parents and children *want* a better relationship. Parents' worst fear is that they may fail as parents. Your parents will not tell you this, for they have too much dignity to maintain.

Besides it would not be good for you to hear it from them. To behold them in helpless anxiety over whether you are going to "turn out well" would shake your confidence in them as well as in yourself.

On the other hand, children feel guilty when they have conflicts with their folks. This can be true even when you feel you are right and they are wrong. After all, you have been the "little person" and they have been the "big people" for quite a long while. It is sort of implied that parents know best, or at least they should. Besides, there is a commandment that most of us have heard at some time or other—"Honor thy father and thy mother." So as angry as we may be at the moment, we usually end up blaming ourselves for these family spats. Incidentally, your parents also blame *themselves*. It is a natural tendency to blame yourself after your conscience has had time to work on you, even though you would never let anybody know it.

What does it mean—"Honor thy father and thy mother that thou mayest live long on the earth?" What does it mean to *honor* our parents? Honor means to respect them in the position which God has given them in regard to us —to give them the obedience due their position. It does not mean that we must always think they are right. We honor them, says the commandment, that we may live long on the earth. Does this mean that if a person dies early, it is evidence that he did not honor his parents? Or if he lives to a ripe old age, is this evidence that he honored his parents? Obviously not. What is meant here is that stable family living is the foundation for a stable society. As children honor their parents they are contributing to this stable society which in turn contributes to the overall health and well-being of the people in that society. It is the needed structure for wholesome community living.

Parents Need Understanding

There are many books today for parents on how to understand their children—their little ones and big ones. But you should remember that parents need understanding, too. In fact there is a book for young people entitled, *Living With Parents.*[1] After all, your parents are simply the children of other parents. It may help you in understanding them if you consider this.

As one young fellow told me, "When I think about Grandpa—well, then, I think that Dad has done pretty good considering." When the heat of our emotions has died down, it is a good thing to do a little reflecting on what all was involved in the tiff. You may get some insights into what caused your father and mother to act— or react—the way they did. This may help you to understand them better. And understanding leads to forgiveness.

Parents are under a commandment, too. "Fathers, do not provoke your children to anger, lest they become discouraged, but bring them up in the discipline and instruction of the Lord."[2] The Phillips version of the New Testament puts it this way: "Fathers, don't over-correct your children or make it difficult for them to obey the commandment, or they will grow up feeling inferior and

[1] By Grace Sloan Overton. Nashville, Tennessee: Broadman Press, 1954.
[2] Ephesians 6:4

frustrated. Bring them up with Christian teaching in Christian discipline."

Now I think you will agree that even though your commandment is difficult, this one for your parents is, too. As a father I stand humbled before it. We all need forgiveness, for we all have broken the commandment. And this is how I would define a Christian home. It is a home where the spirit of forgiveness reigns between parents and children and children and parents, between parent and parent, between brother and sister, between brother and brother, sister and sister.

It is often surprising what can be done to improve seemingly hopeless family situations. The trouble is that the young people themselves are too often defeatists regarding their own parents. They tend to write them off as hopeless—"You can't do anything with *my* mother, not *her!*" This very attitude helps to keep things the way they are. It leaves no room for faith. Perhaps your home is one big battleground. Even this condition has some merit to it. As one young married woman said, "In my husband's family everybody says what he thinks. They have lots of fights but they get over it quickly. In my family we had no fights. Anything emotional was taboo. As a result it was kept inside. I think this is worse."

She has a point. However, just the fact that a fight is out in the open does not mean it will have a healthy effect. Sylvia came to see me after battling with her parents for over an hour straight. She was terribly distraught.

"Oh, how I wish I could avoid these blowups," she said. "I feel so wretched afterward."

"Guilty?" I asked.

"Yes," she said. "They throw it up to me so—that I'm

disrespectful and all that. Also that I have a lousy disposition. I know I have an awful tongue when I get started. I vow I'll never do it again. But I do it anyhow—over and over."

After a while Sylvia's guilt began to dissipate and the original anger took its place. "It's hard not to argue," she said. "I get all upset anyhow and hard feelings result."

"What is the trouble about?" I asked.

"They won't let me go out on dates the way other girls my age do. It sets me dead against them. I hate it when they don't trust me. It makes me so that I don't trust them."

"Is it both your mother and your father?"

"Well, it's mother mostly. Dad goes along with her. We just don't hit it off. I've honestly tried, but my efforts have failed."

"Makes you discouraged."

"She's always so critical of others—like the mothers of my girl friends. Hmmph! Look at the mess she's made out of me! I'm so sick and tired of feeling miserable about half of the time."

"You feel it's her fault."

"She's never trusted me. If I wasn't so afraid of what they might do, I'd speak out. I'd just like to tell her that! 'You think you are such a good parent—look at the mess you've made out of me!' "

Some time later when we were conversing again about her problem, Sylvia said, "I have a longing to talk to Mother about these things."

"As you mentioned before—to show her what a mess she's made out of things?" I asked.

"No—not that. I haven't had any desire to do that lately. No, I just want to talk to her. I have a feeling, though, that if I did, I would cry. In fact I feel like crying right now just talking about it."

"You want to tear down this barrier between you, is that it? You want to love her."

Sylvia couldn't say anything because she was trying to keep her emotions under control.

Things still are bumpy at Sylvia's home, but they are better. Sylvia and her mother are at least talking things over like mother and daughter on occasion. Occasionally their fights end in kissing and making up instead of mutual pouting and inner misery. If it could happen in Sylvia's home, it might even happen in yours.

Problems with Brothers and Sisters

Conflicts between brothers and sisters are unavoidable also. If your brother was in your family first and had Mom and Dad all to himself before you came along to spoil things, you could hardly be surprised if he did not always view you with unmixed joy. It is a pretty big thing to have to share your parents, and there is bound to be some jealousy and resentment in the process.

It was Joan's *younger* sister who caused her no end of trouble. Although she was younger by a year and a half, she acted as though she were the older of the two. However, Joan herself can tell how it felt.

"My sister is aggressive," she said. "Naturally an aggressive child gets more attention and admiration from the parents. I feel the competition keenly, particularly since my sister is very cutting toward me."

"She goes after you with vim and vigor," I said.

"She loves to make a fool out of me," Joan said. "Everything I do she criticizes. I couldn't begin to tell the times she has humiliated me before others."

"And how did you cope with all this?"

"When I was smaller I fought back. But I never could win. My mother never stopped her. She just told me I couldn't take it. If I did ignore her it made her all the more furious. She really went after me then."

"She wanted to get a rise out of you."

"I'm afraid all she did was beat me down. By the time we were in our teens I wasn't even in the running."

"You considered yourself beaten."

"I was beaten—depressed and licked," she said. "When I'm criticized I buckle under pretty easy."

"It makes you feel as if you were worthless," I said.

"I'm afraid that's the way I felt much of the time. Even though I resented my sister bitterly, I got to feeling she was right."

"Her opinion of you became your own opinion of yourself."

"I think it's because of this that I was so slow and awkward," she said. "I envied my sister her efficiency and her social abilities. I was the clumsy one—the dumb one—and the clumsier I was, the more I got it; and the more I got it, the clumsier and slower I became."

"And you felt your mother favored your sister."

"She did," Joan said emphatically. "My mother's efficient too. My sister was what she wanted."

"And your dad?"

Joan was slow to answer. "My dad favored me when I was younger. He was most affectionate with me. Maybe he felt sorry for me. But anyhow Mother didn't like it. She talked to Dad—told him he was spoiling me. I found out about this later. So Dad quit. All of a sudden he changed. I couldn't understand what was wrong—what had changed him—what I had done. He was all I had. Life was miserable from then on. I thought maybe it was because I was a girl. I kept wishing I were a boy. I cried a lot in those days—alone in my bedroom."

"How were things outside your home?" I asked.

"School was another fear. I was sick a year when I was six years old, and my sister caught up with me."

"You both were in the same class?"

"Yes," she said. "And she was so much better than I was. When the teacher would lose her patience with me, she would usually say something like—'Why don't you apply yourself like your sister!'"

"I can imagine how this went over."

"I hated the teacher for saying it. I didn't have the desire to try at all then. I don't know why, but my sister has always gone out of her way to hurt me—to make me feel like two cents. She always liked to take things away from me. She even won my little sister's affections away from me. I hated my home. I think I married early just to get away from it."

But Joan did not get away from it. Her husband was critical also. And all the old problems were aggravated again. She felt he reprimanded her as a child. Her husband fitted into her family pattern and therefore she must face the old problems as they now relate to him.

What Joan did not realize at the time, but was slowly beginning to see, was that her sister was not the confident, secure person she thought she was. Confident and secure persons do not have to attack weaker persons to gain satisfaction. Her sister could get upset too. She was a person who could not feel with others because she had never faced her own feelings. As difficult as it was for Joan to comprehend, her sister was actually jealous of her. For one thing, she was jealous of that early attention that Joan received from her father. From then on it was somewhat of a habit. Joan was easy to beat down and so she got it more. When her sister left home and became a little frog in a big pond instead of a big frog in a small pond, she was completely unprepared for the shock. For the first time she knew what it meant to feel as Joan did, and she was lost.

Now as a married woman Joan must do what should have been done before. Perhaps she could not have done it alone. Even now she needs help. But the objective is clear. She must fight her battles instead of running from them. Instead of allowing herself to be beaten down and drawing into defeated silence, she needs to resist openly and actively. She was better off when as a small child she was still able to fight back than she is now. So it is obvious that she has to go back to that point and try again to fight back. Only this time she must not quit. Whether she wins or loses is beside the point. As long as she continues fighting she cannot lose. The minute she quits she cannot win. There is a significant correlation between resisting oppression and confidence. The one begets the other. As Joan begins to see her sister as one who also is weak and fearful, she may grow to evaluate herself with more respect.

Yet these same jealousies and resentments can be needlessly antagonized.

Perhaps you recall the Bible story of Joseph and his brothers. Joseph was a gifted child. This talent alone would have brought him attention. But he was also the first child born to Rachel, the wife whom his father loved best. It was only natural that jealousies over Joseph's favored position would arise among his ten older brothers, who were born to the other wife.

But Joseph did not help things either. Instead of playing down his importance, he gloried in it. He had a dream in which eleven sheaves of wheat all bowed down to one. He told his brothers the dream, and then proceeded to interpret it to mean that he was that one sheaf and his brothers would all bow down to him. You can imagine how this was taken.

Nor did his father help things. He crowned his favoritism by making a beautiful coat, not for all the brothers, but only for Joseph. Nor was this even enough. When his father asked him to see how things were going with his brothers out in the fields, Joseph wore this coat. This was really rubbing it in. So far as the brothers were concerned it was the last straw, and their aroused jealousy led them to seize him and sell him into Egyptian slavery, at the same time feigning his death by covering the hated coat with animal's blood.

Favored or Disfavored

The charge of favoritism goes on. Sometimes it is real and open; most of the time it is unconscious so far as the parents are concerned; and often it exists more in the imagination of the children than in the feelings of the parents. When favoritism does exist it usually comes about quite naturally. One child stands out in the parents' ideals. Perhaps it is the bright child or the aggressive child. He naturally is more active, accomplishes more, and automatically gets more attention.

Sometimes it is not the favored child who is really *favored*. I know one girl, for example, who was sure that her mother favored her sister over her. She could cite instance after instance to prove it. What she did not realize was that she was a very bright child and her sister was average. Sensing the difference between the girls, her mother, wisely or unwisely, tried to hold the bright child down to protect the less gifted.

The danger in this rivalry among children lies in the feelings of inferiority that may develop in those who feel less favored, and in the insensitivity to the feelings of others that may develop in the supposedly favored ones. If these dangers exist in your family let me talk directly to you. If you feel that you are not so gifted as your brother or sister—if you feel inferior to them because you do not seem to please your parents as much as they do—you are looking at yourself through prejudiced eyes. As a person created by God you are much more than the various characteristics by which you are judging yourself inferior. You are undoubtedly overlooking much about yourself that is anything but inferior, simply because you have the idea that certain characteristics are more important than others—or even all-important. This is not only a lopsided way of looking at yourself; it is not only showing disrespect for your own unique personality; it is showing disrespect for the God who created you and who thought enough of you to give Himself for you. Because of God's demonstration of His love for you on the cross of Christ, you can not only come "boldly and confidently before His throne of grace," but can go just as confidently before your fellow young people.

If you are the favored one in your family you probably are not entirely unaware of it. It ought not to take too much imagination for you to realize how this makes your brother or sister feel. Be sensitive to their feelings. Do not rub it in. Rather play down your favored role. Encourage the others to think well of themselves. Not only will you be helping them in their struggle to grow—you will be helping yourself.

Your Other Parent

So far we have talked only about you, your parents, and your brothers and sisters. But there is more to your family. You have a Heavenly Parent. The good news of Christianity is that this Heavenly Parent loves you, even when you feel you are unlovable. Your Heavenly Parent can do you a lot of good in your family relations. You can go to Him about your problems with your earthly parents. Tell Him how it seems to you. He wants us to be honest with Him.

You may not find this easy. It is difficult to be honest with God even as it is to be honest with people. We are afraid He cannot take it—or cannot take us—if we are. There are also times when it is difficult for us to recognize our bad feelings. We would be shocked if we knew how many we had.

This was Bill Hadley's experience. He came to see me because he was disgusted with himself. He felt he was not accomplishing anything. It was soon apparent that his concern over himself was closely associated with his feelings toward his mother. He wanted to please her more than anything else, and he felt guilty about letting her down. She had sacrificed much in raising him and had reminded him of this at intervals. Now she was sickly and ailing most of the time.

Bill shuddered to think what would happen to him inside if she should die. The more he talked, the more he became slightly critical of his mother. Maybe if she would be more encouraging rather than complaining, he would do better. But as soon as this would come out, he quickly retracted it all by defending her. When he left he looked a little disturbed. I encouraged him to share his feelings with God in prayer.

When he returned the next week he said: "I was mad at you when I left here last time."

"Why was that?" I asked.

"That was it. I didn't know why either. But now I think it was because you were getting too close. I was feeling things I didn't want to feel—or think."

"What, for instance?"

"Let me tell you what happened first. As I said, after I left here I was angry but didn't know why. I had a few more frustrations that day, and by night I was fit to be tied. For some reason I remembered what you said about prayer. I started to let it out. I'm glad I was by myself because it really came. I found myself shouting—first at you, and then at my mother. Yet all the time I was conscious of praying. Man! I didn't know it was that much!"

"I guess it stored up inside of you because you didn't want to face it."

"I don't think I could ever have said those things to you," he said. "But when I was alone—with God—then I could do it. Or rather I should say that I couldn't hold it back. I thought I loved my mother. But I had hate for her too."

"Did you feel guilty about this hate?"

"Well—yes, I did. But it came out so fast that my guilt didn't stop it. It felt good really to get it out. I believe God understands. At least things have been going better since."

"You notice a change," I said.

"I feel relieved," he said. "I think I'll have a better

relationship with my mother for having my eyes opened to my real feelings toward her. I have found it easier to be more honest with her too, even if she doesn't like it. I think things will be better for being more open. One thing for sure, I feel more relaxed around home now."

God is someone different from and other than our parents. Sometimes we get the idea that He is simply an enlarged picture of our earthly parents, and so automatically on their side. He is called a Father, not because He is like human parents but because human parents are to be like Him. We know what God is like by thinking of Him in terms of Jesus, who told us, "He that hath seen me hath seen the Father."

Perhaps you do not feel you know how to pray. Or perhaps you do not feel right in praying. The only way to learn to pray is actually to begin praying. In prayer we learn only by doing. God wants you to come to Him. The central message of the Christian faith is that God has come to us so that we can come to Him. He comes to us as a person. You belong in His presence. All your unworthiness has been taken care of by God Himself on the cross of Christ. So talk to Him as you would talk to the most understanding, forgiving person you can imagine. For that person is God.

You will find that sharing yourself this way with God helps you to grow. It is *the* personal relationship of your life that gives meaning to all of your personal relationships. It gives meaning and purpose to your whole life. It orients all of you, including your sexual nature, toward wholesome and healthy experience. It does this because it orients all of your personality toward Him who is the Creator, Redeemer, and Sustainer of life.

God understands both us and our parents. He is their

parent also, and the parent of our brothers and sisters. Each of us in the family can go to Him to talk things over. It can be truly amazing what this relationship can do for us.

Janice had a nice personality. Everybody liked her. As I grew to know her, I realized that she was a genuinely happy and enthusiastic person. Yet Janice came from a home that offered her none of these qualities. In fact, there was so much hatred in her home that she was forced to leave. How then can we explain Janice? I asked her that. It was rather embarrassing for her to answer, but she managed.

"It's true what you say about my background. But when I was a little girl the neighbors took me to Sunday school. There I learned to know my Heavenly Father. It seems that He has made the big difference."

Prime the Pump

Like Janice, you can talk your family problems over with God. After you have done so you will be more able to cope with these problems. You may even be able to *prime the pump*. Your parents are older than you and it is harder for them to begin a change. You begin. Your parents, too, want respect. They want to think that you like them, look up to them. (So, by the way, do your brothers and sisters, regardless of how they may hide it!) Can you give them some evidence that you do like them? Do not expect them to show immediate joy. They may not even look as though they like it. But down deep underneath they do. They do because they are human beings, just as you are.

I do not mean that you should lose your individuality in trying to please them. This would do neither you nor them anything but harm. Rather, I mean that you should try to work things out with them by showing understanding of how they feel. In the midst of our differences we can continue to be kind, and perhaps, with enough practice, even pleasant. Show consideration to the others. This is your *agape* coming through. It promotes that good feeling in the home that brings out the best from everybody. All of us have a way, after a time, of reacting in kind. So it is to be hoped that consideration and understanding from you will stimulate the same from the others, here and there, now and then.

When our family relationships improve, we are helping not only our future relationships but our own emotional health. God has made us as people with feelings. We have a need both to give and to receive affection. When this is lacking in our family relationships our own nature voices its protest. One way that we may experience this protest is in agitated sexual desires, because God designed our sexual nature as the means for the experience of affection in its deepest meaning. But when our normal need for affection is being met, our sexual desires are more amenable to discipline.

Maybe you feel that your family situation is beyond your ability to remedy. We all have to accept some limitations. You may be right that not much can be done. But this hardly ever means that nothing can be done. And let us do the little something that we can. Let us make the most of what we have. This is a form of accepting ourselves and our situation. For what is acceptance but this— to live positively with the imperfect.

And what if the imperfect means no response? Suppose your efforts to improve your family situation are a total loss? Does this mean *you* are a total loss? Fortunately for you and others like you, life goes beyond parents. In saying this we are not minimizing the loss. We are simply accepting the loss—but not enlarging on it. The greater loss is what our defeat may do to our respect for ourselves.

There have been people who have gone on into adulthood forever trying to establish their worth through searching for parental approval. Theirs is an unending quest for self-acceptance that may never be satisfied simply because the parent involved is too emotionally immature to cooperate. This is tragic. Thank God that in spite of the inestimable value of the parental relationship, our value as persons does not depend on it.

As we have emphasized before, our value as a person is based on the high evaluation that God has placed on each of us. But God does not intend that He should substitute for human relationships. There are others than parents. There is the larger family of humanity. It is not unusual for a person to find what he could not find in his parents in some other older person or group of persons.

Since God does not intend that He should be a substitute for people in our life, He has established the Church. In Christian thinking, God is never separated from the fellowship of believers. Here in the family of God we receive the love and acceptance through which God demonstrates His own love and acceptance. Of course, church groups vary in their ability to fulfill God's intention for them. But on the whole you will receive not only the ties you need but also the opportunities to give of yourself in this fellowship of the Church.

In whatever we do to help ourselves to begin to lay the foundation for our family relationships of the future, we are reminded that our life is not our own—a share of it belongs to our future mate. All that we do should be influenced by this fact.

St. Paul was emphasizing a similar idea when he said. "You were bought with a price. So glorify God in your body." In and through our belonging to others, we belong also to God. When you guide yourself by this thought, you will be motivated from within to make the choices that create a healthy and wholesome personality. The reason for this is obvious. You were created in His image.

When we look at life from the point of view of worshiping the Creator rather than the creature, there can be no hard and fast distinction between things religious and things secular. It is as artificial a cleavage as trying to separate our physical self from our spiritual self. Our life is *one* even as we are one person. We are recognizing today, more perhaps than ever before, the way the different sides of a person's life—social, vocational, recreational, and devotional—all work together. The relationship between the physical and the spiritual, the emotional and the mental, is such that if we neglect one there is trouble for the others, and the person as a whole is the loser. Each of these areas of our life profits from the good care we give to the others. While no one area of our living can substitute for another, it is the spiritual dimension—our fellowship with God—that gives us the sense of values and direction that unites all of our activities into a meaningful whole.

So let us thank God for the good life that He has given us. It is rich and full and ours to enjoy. It is overwhelming in its opportunities and demanding in its obligations. It is a thrilling adventure in faith and hope and love.

Bless the Lord, O my soul: and all that is within me, bless His holy name. Bless the Lord, O my soul, and forget not all His benefits.

STUDY AND DISCUSSION GUIDE FOR
GOD, SEX AND YOUTH
for use by
CHURCH YOUNG PEOPLE'S GROUPS

Preparation for Leaders

The book will be divided into a series of six programs. For these programs there should be several leaders. These leaders should be selected from among the older youth of the Young People's group or even from the young adults of the congregation. Discuss the specific local problems that exist in the area of sex and dating. What do the youth of the congregation need most to receive from their Church in this area?

The leaders will also serve as discussion group leaders—the number of smaller groups depending upon the size of the large Group. If there are six to ten persons in the Group, the Group is the discussion group; if twelve to twenty—two groups, etc. The purpose of the discussion is to encourage each young person to express his own feelings, ideas and problems in the area of the presentation that preceded it. The leader should avoid corrective tendencies, encourage the timid, restrain the aggressive, tie things together, keep the discussion upon the subject at hand, and summarize in conclusion.

Preparation for the Group

Not only the leaders but also the Group should make the decision to have such a program. Therefore there should be an introductory meeting to present the idea of this series and to get the reaction. When the Group's interest appears to have been aroused, let the members discuss the idea in small groups and bring forth questions they would like to discuss in such a series. After the Group has reconvened the leader may write the questions put forth by the groups on the blackboard.

Since frankness, reverence and maturity are necessary for the discussion, the leader may ask the Group whether they can discuss in this spirit. He should particularly draw them out on maturity, suggesting that some evidences of immaturity may be giggling, distractive joking, horseplay, all of which indicate discomfort and embarrassment over the subject. Does the Group have the maturity to discuss this subject?

If all seems to be positive, the leader may then read an interview from the book in order to get identification with the subject. After this he may assign the pages to be read for the first meeting of the series, and urge the Group to attend all of the meetings in order to get the full benefits.

Division of Material

1. Chapters 2 and 3. Stress the essential goodness of sex and the problems encountered in going steady.

2. Chapters 4 and 5. Stress the importance of respect for others in the Christian view of sex and the difference that exists between individuals in this respect.

3. Chapters 6 and 7. Stress the positive—that such problems can be helped if we know how to come to grips with them in ourselves and in others. In contrast to the other presentations, this presentation should be in general terms leaving the specific issues for the small group discussions.

4. Chapters 8 and 9. Emphasize the value of developing much in common outside of the expression of affection in courtship for the benefit of sex in marriage. Stress the blessings and risks of marriage and relate them to the group's present situation and development.

5. Chapters 10 and 11. Emphasize the fact that working on family and personal problems now is the best possible investment for a happy marriage and family in the future.

Structure

1. Have variety in the methods of presentation. Do anything but read—except when dramatizing. The following are some suggestions.

 a. Have the leader review the contents of the assignment and give his reactions.
 b. Have a panel of three leaders giving sections of the assignment and then commenting or raising questions about these sections among themselves.
 c. Have a dialogue between two leaders concerning the contents.
 d. Have an adult—the pastor, the sponsor—present the program, particularly for the section on the marks of affection.
 e. Dramatize the section by acting out some of the interiews recorded in it.
 f. For the section on marriage have an articulate happy married young couple of the congregation present the contents and react to them from their own personal experience.

2. When the subjects of Sex in Solitude and Sexual Abnormalities are discussed (program #3) it is wise to have the school psychologist or local psychiatrist or otherwise the most capable adult in the community present—as the one who presents the program or at least acts as an advisor to the program. It is obviously important that this presentation be done tactfully and with good taste.

3. It is better to arrange the small groups for discussion beforehand so that a balance in the group will be insured. Keep these same groups each time with the same leader, with the exception of program #3 on sexual abnormalities, when it is better to divide in two groups of boys and girls alone. It is also important to select a capable leader for this particular discussion, a woman for the girls, a man for the boys. These discussion groups begin after the presentation of the topic.

4. The leader should raise questions at the close of his presentation to stimulate the discussion groups. Questions which the Group itself has raised beforehand can be brought in at this time.

General Guides

1. Make every presentation personal and related to present events in the life of each youth.

2. Avoid becoming biological or psychological in emphasis. Stay with the religious approach.

3. Mention all references to the Scriptures in *God, Sex and Youth* so that the group can see the relationship of the Word of God to the subject.

4. Be concerned about influencing attitudes as well as ideas. Emphasize respect for others, commitment to God in all that one does, acceptance of oneself as a sexual being with sexual attractions and sexual feelings—as part and parcel with our personality and our growth.

Specific Problems

1. What if there is disruptive behavior because of nervousness over the subject even after the attempt to prevent this in the introductory meeting? Go along with it as much as possible and try to direct it in some way to the subject so that it appears as a legitimate contribution, in the hope that the disruptive youth will adjust to his new role.

2. What about the guilt feelings that arise over previous misconduct? Stress the role of forgiveness—not as an abstract idea but as the love of God that enables one to do better now and to overcome the consequences in the future. This is most effectively done in program #2, on the marks of affection. Perhaps it is best for the pastor to do this.

3. Make the opportunity available for private consultations on these subjects with the adult leaders and the pastor.